Troublesome Country

"Let's Live Up To America's Creed,
For Man Cannot Long Live
By Bunk & Bombs Alone"

*   *   *

by James Hufferd

ProgRESSive

2013

Troublesome Country

WHY WE NEED TO LIVE UP TO OUR CREED:
A HISTORY OF WAR, INJUSTICE AND GREED

Copyright 2010-2013 © by James Hufferd
Published September, 2013 by ProgressivePress.com.
ISBN 1-61577-621-4, EAN 978-1-61577-621-4
Length: 52,000 words, 147 pages, 6 x 9 in., with index.
List Price: $12.95.

BISAC Subject Area Codes:
HIS036000   History / United States / General
POL007000 Political Science / Political Ideologies / Democracy
SOC031000 Social Science / Discrimination & Race Relations
POL045000 Political Science / Colonialism & Post-Colonialism

Troublesome Country is a forceful statement of what is right about America — as well as a history of where we've gone wrong. Our principles are the best the world has ever known. Yet failure to live up to our creed leads time and again to great wrongs — from the genocide of the Indians, slavery, and discrimination, to rule by corporations, the privatization of our currency, serial undeclared wars for empire, increasing inequality, and the erosion of rights under the surveillance state. With an array of fascinating, little-known details, the author shows how each failure comes from betraying our ideals, and calls for us to finally live up to them.

Americans overwhelmingly agree with and take pride in the ideals inherited from our Revolutionary founding era. Throughout our history, however, we have routinely done precisely the *opposite*. *Troublesome Country* presents an unflinching evaluation of America's true history, witnessing a generation-after-generation stupendous failure to put into practice our cherished national ideals. This book is a measuring-standard challenging us that this failure is the cause of our national decay, which is now so conspicuous to all. The cure is for our citizens to begin to live up to our vociferously-professed ideals *en masse*, and to relentlessly hold to account our governing bodies and institutions to truly serve and represent our deeply-held ideals: **popular rule** or democracy, **freedom, equality, justice,** and **independence**.

...To everyone

THE AMERICAN CREED

I, as an American, believe that the direction of our government on all matters should be routinely determined by the people, in accordance with the people's judgment. I believe that the government cannot legitimately control the people's behavior or disposition. I believe that our laws should be applied to all equally. I believe that the pursuit of justice is a mandate and not an option, to be served with uniform diligence and due process. I believe that the American people as individuals as well as the American nation, being richly endowed, should live independently, and not depend on financial overlords. And I demand that all due measures be undertaken to perpetually and fully achieve these conditions and ends, and that all contrary be ceased.

(*__Democracy__* – *__Freedom__* – *__Equality__* – *__Justice__* – *__Independence__*)

(Signed) _____

Contents

Part 1 – The Greatest Creed on Earth – *Ours!*

Does a nation have a purpose? One that defines its life, distilled into a strongly held, deeply felt consensus *creed* informing and guiding its highest aspirations, or at least purporting to shape its thrust of action across centuries? Does America subscribe to the *defining creed* necessarily attending such a purpose? I believe that, in our mind and our rhetoric, it clearly does. Our creed, I submit, consists of *five inseparable sentiments* instilled by our education and assumed unquestionably and proudly by the overwhelming majority of us as our nation's highest ideals. These sentiments or doctrines we commonly deem more than worth living and fighting for. *Our creed*'s components are as follows:

1. Freedom to control the government. This is the idea that the direction of the government should be freely determined by the people.

2. Freedom from government control. This is the idea that the government cannot legitimately control the people's behavior, at least as long as we do not harm others or, in our common free perception, endanger ourselves.

3. All men (all humans) are created equal. This is the idea that our laws be applied to us all equally.

4. Liberty and justice for all. This is the idea that justice is not merely an option, but a mandate, and is to be served by uniform due process.

5. Personal as well as national independence. The American people, being richly advantaged by nature, should live largely independently.

Throughout the many generations that have successively refined and established America's compact five-fold purpose expressed in the American *creed* since its inception, a kaleidoscope of circumstances have shaped, defined, and tested all of the facets of the core, or nuclear, national mind. At each and every turn, the challenges confronting and developing our purpose have been unrelentingly stern from quarters and sources that coveted exclusively for themselves *the nation's* sovereignty and benefits.

Those unstinting, exclusively selfish interests have emerged victorious to an unnerving, and at times almost total, extent. Thus have strong concentrations of power sought without stint, repeatedly, to strip away and claim the mantle of sovereignty bequeathed to *all* of the people, as stipulated in the ideals of the heartfelt creed, basic to our Constitution – as the chapters ahead reveal.

The successful outcome of the struggle that needs yet to be joined strongly for clear *national sovereignty*, even now usurped by overwhelmingly powerful combinations, is increasingly in doubt.

Hence, the generation now emerging is faced with the murky challenge of recovering our promised birthright. For the benefit of all Americans, they must see the way clearly in order to redeem our loss of universally beneficial purpose and fulfill the *creed,* so heartily evoked by Lincoln's *"government of the people, by the people, and for the people." All* parts of that most inspired formula will have to be redeemed to recover the nation we cherish.

Some may object that we don't even have an *official* American creed. That's true. Although we do not have an *official language* in the U.S., English is our *national* language – spoken and written to varying degrees of aptitude by almost all of us. Just so, we *do* have what clearly amounts to a *national creed* – and it is at least basically as I have laid it out here.

Others may object that we need to add tenets to our creed. For instance: *"Competition."* Ready to operationalize it for all, fair and free? *Then, let's level the field!* And, could there be *additional* tenets that would be enthusiastically embraced by virtually all Americans? Then, *list away!*

And so, if we can assume our *creedal* list is fairly accurate, the relevant question becomes, *how have we done*, generation by generation, at *implementing* this *nearly universally agreed-upon creed* we have hewn for ourselves and passed down? How strong have been our positive thrusts, so defined? How strong and threatening or destructive have been our narrower-interest push-backs?

In so many words: how can we realistically rate ourselves before the world in the vaunted category of proven character?

And in what, if any part or parts, do we actually excel? In what parts do we still have a wealth of determined work and care to invest in order to live up to our ambitious and unique social contract, in order to present before the world the exceptional reality we are so eager to endlessly boast of?

Thank heaven our history is not yet over! Let us first see how we have done so far. In the chapters ahead, we will air and discuss a curious, infuriating, and intolerable fact. We will find a *nearly unbroken, centuries-long record of uniform denial, betrayal, and evasion of every principle we claim to believe in,* which this country was founded on and emphatically (and loudly) claims to represent. We will discover that this shocking pattern of forsaking our sworn "ideals" in practice is broken only by an *occasional* notable and heroic exception, one who briefly and bravely upholds those cherished principles – the very tenets of our national creed and soul of what we mean by "America" and "American".

The most encouraging gains and victories we can cite in this regard – and there are, of course, many over the years –end up getting lost and overwhelmed among all the accumulating stinging nettles that continue to crop up around them. So, despite every advantage, our record is, in fact, *inexcusably dismal*. And if we, as individuals, haven't grossly betrayed America's beloved *creed* (our most cherished ideals and principles) ourselves, we've stood by and watched.

It must be asked, would honesty and courage in facing up to that disheartening record of betrayal of self and mankind mean one hates his (her) country? *Use your God-given brain!*

It may be that we're now, effectively, to the point where *even reading this book* will constitute an act of courage. But, take its message in from some source and take it to heart: *America must!* To succeed as a nation, we must acknowledge our stunningly thorough betrayal and subversion of our very foundational *creed* of resolved beliefs; we must *turn that betrayal around* by resolving to put *into effect* the principles of our own sacrosanct making and affirmation – *what we say we stand for.*

Let the shrinking violets, the cowards and the incorrigible cynics look away. True Americans must *do* something! Seriously rededicate and fiercely adhere anew, and the rot that troubles us so and that drags us down will *die!* If we fail to adhere to these words and renew, it will most likely be *our demise* in these accelerating, brutal days. At the very least, it will ensure our equally tragic metamorphosis into something else.

Starting today, renounce and refuse to tolerate our and our leaders' schizoid, *"end justifies the means"* excuses. From this day forward, *live* as one re-united people – *personify America's unmatched creed! That* is our solution, the solution the vast majority of us long for!

Part 2 – A.B.C.: America before the Creed – Colonial Times to 1776

The creed did not come to America early.

Perhaps everyone knows by now, however vaguely, that Christopher Columbus was not by a long shot the first far-traveler to reach America. The "Indians", of course, came first of all by far, as far as we know.

But then, they had it relatively easy, we hasten to remind ourselves, because they are thought to have come dry-shod overland in the far north, which didn't require too much grey matter, just a steady and determined plodding, one foot ahead of the other – surely no great feat. And, of course, we can't forget that the Spanish conquerors of Mexico in the sixteenth century showed so little regard for signs of non-European intelligence that they endeavored to destroy every Native American (Mayan) book they could get their hands on.

That the Vikings came early seems almost by accident, accomplished merely by following the closely aligned stepping stones of the Arctic across, only looking for something to plunder, a little grass for their livestock and fields to grow a few stalks of hearty grain. And they probably didn't stay very long. Of course, the Vikings were Europeans, so they did have, we can rest assured, at least some brainpower and a synapse or two of imagination inside those helmets. So goes our usual thinking.

Early arrivals by others – mainly European – are recorded in passing or just rumored. So they don't concern anybody very much but a few scholars seeking to justify their own existence by spying or scying inscriptions or scratches, or whatever they are, on relics, dredging up stories long and probably as well forgotten, and for good enough reason, so the thinking goes. A cloud of deniability shrouds the lot of them, although some perhaps might rest at least lightly on bedrock of fact.

But when the claims, well-anchored in evidence or not, point to a full-fledged earlier non-European crossing or discovery, our literati seem to grow just a bit uneasy, not to say unglued exactly, immediately imputing cults and baseless legends for the claims before thoroughly processing the evidence, be whatever it may.

Thus, the claims of a retired Brit sea captain named Gavin Menzies in recent years to have traced the progress of a Chinese imperial fleet around the earth on a 1421 voyage, leaving tiny colonies and traces, have fared less than well with the pros.[1]

An interesting and charming follow-up volume to Menzies' was produced by a Canadian architect, claiming to have discovered evidence of one of these Chinese globe-trotting expedition's settlements, on a hilltop on his native Cape Breton Island.

Evidence cited includes some enticing perceived parallels between aspects of the unique culture of the region's Mic-maq Indians and that of Chinese minority peoples. But this author's claims (like Menzies') didn't cut it at all with the professional archaeologists, who only belatedly and, it seems, reluctantly checked out the hilltop site.[2]

Meanwhile, the scenario put forward by Guyanese writer Ivan Van Sertima, among others, over the course of several volumes and years, that West Africans had crossed the Atlantic to Central America repeatedly far earlier in reed vessels, may or not have been accurate.

There apparently is, though, evidence in pre-Columbian Meso-American plastic art, painstakingly collected by German noble Alexander Von Wuthenau over many years, that black Africans were not unknown in the region. Meanwhile, Van Sertima claims have met with near unanimous dismissal and ridicule a priori. The shaping of the New World, it appears, must be left exclusively to Aryans.[3]

A negatively influencing strain of nineteenth century thought known as "Aryanism" infects much of our history and provides the textual background for the blatantly bigoted "white supremacy" movement.

And the Indians, who we have to concede came earlier, didn't achieve very much by way of advances or lasting influences, especially north of Mexico, it is often openly or tacitly agreed. When the Vikings landed and at least briefly settled on the North American coast, two full generations before William the Conqueror invaded England, they were looking for hardy grazing and crop land, and seem to have been beset by the Skraelings (Indians and, to the north, Inuit), who evidently didn't want them around for some reason. They left

---

[1] Gavin Menzies, *1421, The Year China Discovered America*, (London: Transworld, 2002, New York: Harper- Collins, 2003).

[2] Paul Chiasson, *The Island of Seven Cities, Where the Chinese Settled When They Discovered America*, (New York: St. Martins, 2007).

[3] See Léon Poliakov, *The Aryan Myth*, (New York: Barnes & Noble, 1974, pp. 272-277, et al. A particularly virulent elite branch of the same poisoned tree is "British Israelitism," which purports to confer the divine favor granted to Israel in the Hebrew scriptures to the British and their far- flung spawn, as natural descendants identified by the cult as the "Lost Tribes". See Anton Darms, The Delusion of British Israelitism, (London: Publications Office, "Our Hope," 1938).

absolutely no legacy, it appears, unless the gene for blue eyes, reported passed down in a couple of instances.

But Columbus wasn't even next, all evidence indicates. Yet, the question remains unresolved: then, who was? Madoc the noble Welshman? Brendan the Irish mariner/cleric? Some taciturn fisher folk from Bristol? Or perhaps someone even more unidentifiable?

The point is that no one before Columbus managed to set off quite the endless chain of publicity, pugnacity, positioning, pseudo-piety, presumption, profiteering, plunder, pleasure-seeking, or parochial self-congratulation that he did. It's been enough to have rocked and revolutionized both the New World and the Old non-stop ever since, keeping us all perpetually on the brink of interminable chaos and yearning for peace.

What was it that Columbus sought? Gold and Asian spices for his Italian food – because he fully intended to be and just assumed the whole time he was hereabouts, finding "America", that he was in Asia.

Van Sertima, the champion of African pre- Columbian crossing and activity in America, tells us that his theory, regardless of its merits or the evidence, suffered from scholars' almost-universal revulsion at the thought that "flat-nosed Africans" could cross the mighty ocean before the "'discoverer' Columbus, a man blessed with expert geographical knowledge and navigational skills". Who was "so blessed indeed that he believed at first be had stumbled on the backside of India, that Cuba was the continent, South America an island, and the Caribbean See [sic] the Gulf of the Ganges."[4]

The Portuguese knew how to sail to Asia, and did. Columbus's own colony, among the Tainos on the north side of Santo Domingo, lasted barely five years. Five years of hell for the Tainos.[5]

But, his gold fever became permanently established in the European bloodstream, and mariners spent the next two-plus centuries trying to find their way through and around the impenetrable, infernal thicket of banal dullness – ordinary virgin land – that stood in the way, to get on to the real prize, Asia. Thus, Columbus it was who started the whole picture-show following a long series of insubstantial and meaningless flits and flickers in the dark at the start.

As far as the five factors or tenets we have identified as making up the American creed, all given at least lip service almost universally today, there

---

[4] Ivan Van Sertima, *Early America Revisited*, (New Jersey: Transaction Publishers, 1998).
[5] See Kathleen Deegan and José Maria Cruxent, *Columbus's Outpost Among the Tainos: Spain and America at La Islabels, 1493 – 1496*, (New Haven: Yale Press, 2002).

was no evident sign of any of them as yet. No seeds were planted that could have led to them in the soil of the New World, and mentally and culturally, none of the forefathers of their development had ever even left Europe, or probably anywhere else they eventually might have come from, in this whole long, young, restless, and now remote period.

A curious, but not irrelevant, side note is that, following the consequential discovery of the New World by a man who was apparently Italian sailing for Spain and the arrival of another Italian, Giovanni Caboto (John Cabot) sailing for England in the late-15th century, there were no permanent English settlements (forerunners of the vast later Anglo-American empire) planted in the New World for over a century – four or five generations – down to 1607.

Why? Because hit-and-run exploitation and navigation through the conceptually wafer-thin barrier of North America were simply the fashion of the day. And the natives, only lightly regarded – persuaded to set fishing nets, supply fleeting day-labor, directions, and so forth – were quite ignored. There was vanishingly little interest by anyone in belonging to the land as a citizen or anything else, and few of the participants possessed even the least bit of education or, seemingly, curiosity.[6]

The ships dispatched by Sir Walter Raleigh to Carolina in the 1580s regarded the Sound between the Outer Banks islands that they discovered and the continent – too wide to see across in a couple of places – as more likely than not the beginning of the Pacific Ocean, and were busy practicing their lines to trade successfully with the wily and refined East Asians, while scouting up and down the shore for sampans and rickshaws.

That the Raleigh colony on Roanoke Island (late 1580s) didn't last was apparently due to a lack of success at cultivating neighborly relations with the native settlements.

The first long lasting or permanent (although miniscule) English settlements on land that much later became the U.S. (along with others nearby were French) were undoubtedly fish drying and net-repairing stations on islands off of Maine. And these led eventually to the establishment of the more serious settlement in the same vicinity known as Sagadahoc, or the Thayer colony, in mid-1607, a couple of months after the vaunted first permanent English New World settlement at Jamestown on the James River in what is now the state of Virginia.

---

[6] There was some fancying afoot. Norumbega was the odd-sounding name of a fabulous fanciful kingdom – complete with maps – unvisited, but thought to exist within the vast interior of the Northeast. See Emerson W. Baker, *American Beginnings: Exploration, Culture, and Cartography in the Land of Norumbega*, (Lincoln: Univ. of Nebraska Press, 1995).

The generally-considered-positive result of all of this was the expansion of European horizons and a presumed new beginning of wisdom. But the collateral breakage in the process, from self-absorption and arrogance, was already well under way.

Nor did the settlers coming to shape the sunrise outer fringe of sand and rocks along the Atlantic over the next several generations display much of anything of the later five-fold American creed, our unwritten social contract and promise to one another.

There was no (or virtually no) "all men created equal" prospect, no "justice for all," no "freedom from community control," most certainly no "freedom to control the government" – really, quite the opposite. And the aura of "independence" pertained only by virtue of sheer distance from the source country, and not from any such political will. The stage was only starting to be set. America had most certainly not yet been conceived, let alone birthed.

Mythology has inevitably played a major errant (or negative) role in producing the America that eventually came to be, from nothing really tangible.

Throughout the whole sixteenth century, the Spanish were busy founding posts and charting maps in the sunnier climes down below, and the French, English, possibly Basque, and Portuguese fisher folk were plying the bays and inlets more to the north.

Meanwhile, errant travelers as far as we know only from Europe – Verrazano, Hudson, Champlain, Estevan Gomes – were poking their heads into estuaries on the long, quiet stretch of coast in between, inquiring after the reported settled and rich Norumbega, supposedly replete with oranges and almonds, silk and silver, geese and gold, and rumored to begin just above tidewater.

The middle latitudes – eventually independent – lay improbably open and unclaimed, and no one came as yet to settle there. Instead, grab and run was still the rule. Everything was flimflam in earliest not-yet-America – with nothing established, no one to stay and put down roots along the whole of the long, illusive, savage New World shore.

*   *   *

A consortium (or conspiracy) of eight wealthy investors in London, desiring to change all that and establish what would be a permanent English trading colony in the middle of the facing American coast sought a royal charter at the start of the new seventeenth century, for a venture they christened the "Virginia Company." King James I in 1603 granted them their charter, shrewdly splitting these eight applicant adventurers into two sets: the "Virginia Company of London," to colonize what is now the Virginia shore, and the "Virginia Company of Plymouth," to found a colony at Sagadahoc in what is now Maine, both in the summer of 1607.

One of the eight, Edward-Maria Wingfield, was singularly instrumental in getting the enterprise and its approval moving again after languishing for several years. He was responsible, too, for recruiting about 40% of the company's 105 original colonists, only 28 of whom survived the first winter.

Wingfield was also the only one of the original investors to cross the Atlantic to Virginia himself to launch the venture on the ground. For this, he is sometimes distinguished as the real founder of Virginia and of English colonization in what would become the United States. His contribution is all the more important realizing that the French or Spanish would surely have taken the ground had it not been for this adventurous Wingfield's boldness and dispatch. It was he who selected the Jamestown site for its defensive characteristics, and served a stormy stint as the unruly colony's first "president" – occasionally construed as making him the real first president of (or, really, in) the United States![7]

But, what of the infinitely more-famous Captain John Smith's place and role as founder? Alexander Brown, who wrote a definitive history of America's origins a century ago, comments tersely that "Smith's so-called History of Virginia is not a history at all; but chiefly a eulogy of Smith and a lampoon of his peers."[8] It was Smith's own depiction that set his place. And, we are reminded that "In English History, when once a belief is established, either as to the worth or worthlessness of a person or a profession, this becomes a fixture."[9] True.

The Sagadahoc Colony, established much to the north at the same time, didn't survive many brutal Maine years of cold, but undoubtedly was preceded by earlier fishing posts on islands nearby, some still settled today, though their early residents were unlikely scribblers.

Officers of the Virginia Company in London would seem to have held a certain amount of inexplicable regard for the opinions and rights of ethnically diverse peoples. Whether this sentiment extended to a shared conviction with much-later subscribers to America's national creed, that "All men are created equal," is doubtful.

---

[7] Jocelyn R. Wingfield, *Virginia's True Founder, Edward-Maria Wingfield and His Times*, (Book Surge, 2007), p. 1.
[8] Alexander Brown, *Genesis of the United States*, (Nabu Press, (New York: Houghton-Mifflin, 1897), II, 1010.
[9] E.M. Tenison, *Elizabethan England*, (Leamington Spa, 1947), Volume viii, p. 22.

But, the President and Council of the Jamestown Colony, Mr. Wingfield et al, were, notably, instructed in 1607: "…in all your passages, you might have great care not to offend the naturals, if you can eschew it."

Of course, the instruction implies that if they must offend or prejudice "the naturals" in the course of accomplishing their purpose, they are to proceed to get the job done. But then, isn't it always understood, among the civilized, that if the locals are opposed to what you want to do, you must, reluctantly perhaps, act to get rid of the "threat"?

Not always, actually. As one example, the instruction issued to agents in the field by Colonel Cândido Mariano da Silva Rondon of the old-time Brazilian Indian Protection Service was the opposite: "Die if you must, but kill never." So, there is latitude, at least logically, available for adopting an emphasis on equality and life as the primary objective in all instances. Would our country be a different place if we had always insisted on living by this element of our own creed? Yes. Better.

From the cradle, we are taught that the Pilgrims of Plymouth Colony and Plymouth Rock originated and exemplified America's creedal values. In stable family units, yes, it is true. Yet, overwhelmingly, those doughty patriarchs would have been repulsed by the notion of equality, meriting anything like equal justice and shared enjoyment of freedom involving them and their own women and representatives of darker races. Also, and perhaps even more to the point, they were communitarians, violently hostile, in the main, to libertarian or dissenting lifestyles and philosophies.

These pilgrims and pilgrim spawn spread themselves widely, but remained throughout their age essentially European sectarians who wanted to be separate in their own like-minded communities, and were in no wise the distinctive, individualistic Americans who became characteristic later. That "earlier Founding Fathers" rubric is hogwash, largely embraced by those in demand of a certain caste of religious forebears.

What, then, turned such as these into opportunistic Yankees, hawk-nosed and sharp-eyed in seeking every (arguably) fair-minded advantage, by the next century, the seed-people of a far-flung strain of developers moving westward? Both flinty land and rich sea, time, and far-flung markets to supply. And the appreciation they gained of what individual hard work and thrift could accomplish led them to disdain sloth and reliance on slave labor and favor, in due time, the course of abolitionism. But, with America's creedal ideals they did not start out.[10]

---

[10] See Richard L. Bushman, From Puritan to Yankee, Character and the Social Order in Connecticut, 1690-1765, (New York: Norton, 1970).

In the realm of deeds, as opposed to beliefs, seventeenth-century New England was so diametrically opposed to the spirit as well as the letter of what would later become the tenets of the American creed as to make it a sort of shatter-zone of horrendous, brooding tragedy, involving relations with "the other" –women, Indians, blacks, freethinkers. The reality of life thereabouts quickly became in fact the opposite of our mythic image of harmony, fostered by Norman Rockwell depictions of the First Thanksgiving. And, although many of New England's founders lived interesting and adventurous lives, the contrast between myth and reality in this case could not be more pronounced.

Nor the horrific consequences: a byword, certainly, for the tragedy of our modern failure to live more in sync with our positive and noble ideals.

Nevertheless, for reasons probably unfathomable, Plymouth Rock – the symbol of a primordial, pristine America – has been sold to us as our Rock of Gibraltar … fixed, solid, stalwart. But the comparison between the two rocks in physical terms is apt. Gibraltar the mighty pillar, immovable, guarding the Strait of Hercules. And, Plymouth Rock, a middling erratic boulder viewable down in an access-restricted hole between high tides. Surely, the Blarney Stone is more venerable.

Pilgrim New England was foremost and first a man's world. Generally, men charged with savagely beating their poor wives had only to remind the court that their women were, by their law, their property, and could be treated in any manner at all. The prejudices the community maintained against persons considered less in gender and lesser in race, or its frequent surrogate, religious belief, sometimes competed for primacy (or, rather, lowest place).

In 1697, Hannah Emerson Daston, with her infant of but five days, was kidnapped by Indians – "somehow" angered at losing their lands and by the encroachment of hostile, often murderous new towns in their midst – and forced to march a hundred miles into the wilderness with them. In due time, the wily mother and wife – whose child succumbed to the rigors of the forest air – rose up and murdered all of her captives alike, adults and children, while they slept. More savage than the Indians had been to her, she was generally celebrated for bravery, but two centuries farther on she was lambasted by the novelist Hawthorne and those like him for her murderous vengeance.

Great wars in the 1600s, such as the Pequot War and so-called King Philip's War, which set all of New England ablaze, were brought about by colonial communities' insistence that the native inhabitants accept the Christians' stronger claims to any lands they wanted, at the Indians' expense and loss of their ancestral homes, to hell with their remarkable hospitality and help as a starting point for shaping an accommodation. And likewise, anyone who even read the Christian gospels differently from the "established church's" interpretation and practice would be forced to separate and form a new realm of his own elsewhere.

The founders of Rhode Island and Connecticut had been compelled to leave the mother colony, and likewise that licentious rogue, Thomas Morton of Merrymount, a freethinker – and by some accounts, America's first poet and man of letters. (By other accounts, its first shameless miscreant.) Tolerance, of a certainty, was no Pilgrim virtue.[11]

The other claimant to the title of first poet was, ironically, a woman, Ann Bradstreet. And (the irony grows!) a third noted colonial-era poet, later, but from the same community, Phillis Wheatley – who was not so well-received – was both a woman and a black woman, originally a slave, whom many refused to believe actually wrote the poems published and circulated under her name. And, while celebrated by some of America's Founding Fathers, she could not attract wide support and died in poverty.

Women, generally regarded as objects of temptation and the cause of straying from acceptably bland demeanor and conduct, were the especial targets of the most notorious of early colonial New England's wandering into fanciful flights of scapegoating and superstition, the Salem witch trials. The attached mindless terror generated by unscrupulous leaders grasping for power then is said to have its parallel in our own recent past.[12]

But then, the Pilgrims and their immediate descendents came straight from a European realm (and lived separate here), and they never claimed to embrace the creed that we have proclaimed and pledged to an approving and receptive world.

If the pinch-toe square-buckle Pilgrims were, in fact, the root of one later (and notably troublesome) American strain of human interaction, it is well to remind ourselves that our national makeup is far more cosmopolitan and inclusive than their separatist one.

As historian Russell Shorto put it, "England was [then] on the verge of a century of religious wars that would see royal heads roll and crowds of ordinary citizens flee.[13]

---

[11] Thomas Morton, a friend and protector of Indians, was charged with licentiousness and deported. Another rogue, William Phipps, meanwhile, who had been a notorious pirate earlier in life, was elected to high office because his professed religious views were suitably orthodox.

[12] See Frances Hall, *Such Men Are Dangerous, The Fanatics of 1692 and 2004*, (Hinnesburg, VT: Upper Access, 2004.

[13] Russell Shorto, *The Island in the Center of the World*, (New York: Vintage, 2005), p. 26.

In fact, the Pilgrim religious dissenters themselves had fled. To much more-tolerant Holland, where Catholics and Jews and refugees of all sorts had been accorded asylum by the Dutch Protestants and, if desired, equal citizenship. The Pilgrims had stayed for twelve years before moving on to form their exclusive commonwealth across the waves. (The narrow-toes, it seems, couldn't stand mixing with the tolerant back then, either).

Soon afterward, the Dutch established their own cosmopolitan colony in what became New York, with English colonies as bookend neighbors on the north and south. And there, Dutch settlers were only one of several European nationalities represented, and again, Jews fresh from Holland's recent Brazil fiasco,[14] Catholics, and free blacks were met on the streets, this time of a rustic Manhattan.

When the Restorationist English took over the place from the waning imperial Dutch in 1664, they were wise and impressed enough – like the Chinese taking back Hong Kong over three centuries later – by the plan and panache of the existing city, to take pains to retain both following the takeover.

Hence, has New York grown up as a unique American city, not only larger than others, but proffering its tolerant and inclusive soul to blend in the national mix, at times confounding, and even exasperating, narrower-minded folk.

In the early 1660s, only a blink of an eye before the more-powerful English took over New Netherlands and New Amsterdam from the Dutch, the brand new Province of Carolina was being established by colonists coming to Albemarle Sound from the earlier Virginia settlements and from Great Britain in search of land. At first, there was peace and a treaty with the few Chowamoc Indians thereabout; the rights of all to have a place, respect, and freedom were honored.

In the fall of 1662, an English scout named William Hilton, representing a group of New Englanders, explored the Cape Fear River, not so very far distant, looking for home sites. The New Englanders came down and settled, finding very few natives afoot and not feeling threatened. But, within a few months, almost all of them left and returned north suddenly, abandoning their livestock, apparently following run-ins with hostile Indians.

The next year, Mr. Hilton scoured the land anew, this time representing English from Barbados and more New Englanders wanting to move, whose homesteads soon lined the river for sixty miles.

---

[14] See James Hufferd, *Cruzeiro do Sul, A History of Brazil's Half-Millennium*, Vol. 1, (Bloomington: Author House, 2005), pp. 296-321.

By 1666 and '67, the Indians of the region had gotten incensed at the newcomers, who kept seizing their children and – so they said – sending them to a special school to be favored with Christianity and the rudiments of education. Early glimmerings of the unctuous paternalism that was to dog white-native relations on every continent for centuries to come?

No, worse! The Indian children were, every last one of them as they emerged from the forest, being seized and sold and shipped away into slavery in order to cut off the coming generations.

Fighting determinedly with bows and arrows against the settlers' muskets, the relentless natives again rid that remote stretch of coast of every last settler.[15] Left behind were scornful natives with bitter memories and tales of woe.

And so it mostly went on and on, decade after decade, until well past the end of America's colonial age.

Not too surprisingly, then, our creed, bequeathed to us from our forefathers, would probably not have registered even as much as a single percent approval in that grim pre-dawn.

*   *   *

The germ of the radical idea of incorporating women into mainstream society on equal footing, of accepting Jews and other seeming chronic misfits, and the use of double-entry bookkeeping and other cutting-edge commercial schemes, were gleaned in America from practices already ongoing in Nieu Netherland, the colony appropriated from the greatest trading country in the world in that time. Such grudgingly accepted adaptations represented only the slightest cracking of the English colonists' accustomed disadvantaging patterns. Practices affected included confronting those who were different, segregating groups, ranks, genders, and classes, dominating all, and airtight control.

Slavery, meanwhile, was the virtually unchallenged social norm of the day throughout even the northern New World colonies – including the Dutch settlements. (In the Spanish and Portuguese empires to the south, interestingly, slavery did not go unchallenged, with noted clergymen Las Casas and Antônio Vieira inveighing loudly and early for abolition of the practice). In North America, the clergy – and, after them, everybody else – pointed out that scripture did not explicitly forbid slavery, and even countenanced one believer holding another in bondage, but only counseled forbearance and mild treatment.

---

[15] See E. Lawrence Lee, *Indian Wars in North Carolina, 1663-1763*, (Raleigh: North Carolina Division of Archives and History, 1997).

The first known break in the wall of approval of African slavery in the dominant community came when a group of Quakers living in Germantown, outside of Philadelphia, questioned the practice on moral grounds. Quakers in the city, most of whom owned slaves themselves, were sorely embarrassed. The petition was largely ignored at the time, but provided a precedent for a tremendous amount of anti-slavery pamphleteering in the coming decades.

At the turn of the 1700s, even while the acquisition of African slaves in New England was on the increase, a Massachusetts judge named Samuel Sewall issued a pamphlet entitled "The Selling of Joseph," condemning the institution and equating it to the robbing of the victim. A fellow judge, John Saffin, answered this pamphlet with another, repeating the standard scriptural defense pointing out the omission of a sanction. And there, the argument more or less stuck until long after the Revolutionary War, with words occasionally flying back and forth, pro and con, all the way to Georgia and Spanish/British Florida. After almost a century of this stalemate on the issue, antagonisms had begun to fester on both sides.

But already, its course resembling a giant pendulum, swinging forever back and forth through the canyons of time, the lives and struggles of ordinary and not-so-ordinary men and women were devoted to the monumental issue of slavery. And insolence and sheer meanness were expended aplenty in the process, a ponderous material, as well as moral, stake being involved.

Phillis Wheatley could be viewed as Exhibit A in her time. Arriving in Boston a slave from West Africa at the ripe age 7 or 8 in 1761 on board the schooner Phillis, she appropriated the ship's "pleasing" English name.

A few years later, she emerged from the sheltering household of her master's well-to-do family, a startlingly accomplished poet, polished in English, the classics, and Latin. Her poems were circulated and admired, but – bizarrely – no one seemed to be able or willing to believe they were really of her own authorship. An African, as everyone "knew," lacked the capacity to create genuine literature.

So, her high-toned owner, Mr. Wheatley, invited his social peers, the leading men of Boston and among the most erudite in the whole of colonial America, to come and test her and decide whether she really could have been the author of the poems.

They were shocked to determine that she was; hence, she became widely published and sought after. After the Revolution began, she wrote a poem to celebrate General Washington, winning his admiration and modest thanks.

But, ironically, Thomas Jefferson wasn't ready to buy it. And his reasoning is most interesting. Yes, he conceded, she had been the author. But, the quality of the poems was, inevitably, immature, or so he said. They were imitative, not thoughtful. Such had to be the case. Because, while the black does certainly have a soul and a mind, and is fully human, his (or her) mental capacity is limited, and cannot produce anything of genius.[16] This normally most imaginative Founder would not even conceive of an exception at the time – which is what any poet of genius is, after all!

Phillis Wheatley had, by the early 1770s, become the widely acclaimed Oprah of her day. And thus, many at the base of the early abolition movement, as it turned out – gainsaid even the great Jefferson on this particular verdict. Not a simple man was this Jefferson, who sparked the freedom of so many, but unlike the more solid, less-cerebral Washington, did not choose to free his own slaves even at his death.

Perhaps for reasons similar to Jefferson's, the public could not, by common consensus, quite swallow Phillis' claims; and her poems, although wildly popular in their singular form, could not become regularly published. And the first of them that finally did didn't sell.

So, as Louis Henry Gates put it, when Phillis Wheatley was freed, and removed from the wealthy family's support, it turned out that "freedom had enslaved her to a life of hardship," of just getting by, as a lowly cleaning woman. But, she did leave a legacy: One of her long-lost poems in manuscript sold at auction for $70,000 when it surfaced a few years ago.

So, what exactly did Jefferson actually mean by his most famous and most redolent phrase? Those who revered the gallant and liberating phrase and, at least by implication, the man who penned it, repeatedly asked that question, both before and after his death.

The best answer, it turns out, may be that, in the minds of most, all citizens are created equal, and all who are equally worthy of respect as valid citizens are, indeed, entitled to be treated equally.

But, who would be qualified to be treated equally by inclusion as citizens must be answered over time. The numbers must be fashioned to include all those, and only those, who could demonstrate they belonged.

---

[16] Louis Henry Gates, *The Trials of Phillis Wheatley, America's First Black Poet and Her Encounters with the Founding Fathers*, (New York: Basic Civics, 2003), p. 42. Jefferson's opinion, though, it turned out, was not irrevocably fixed.
In 1791, he responded in a letter to Benjamin Banneker, a black scientist from Maryland who had sent him a copy of the almanac he published: "No body wishes more than I do to see such proofs as you exhibit, that nature has given to our black brethren talents equal to those of the other colours of men..." Lilly Patterson, *Benjamin Bannecker, Genius of Early America*, (Nashville: Pantheon, 1978), p. 114. Jefferson added he had sent the Almanac on to the Secretary of the Academy of Sciences in Paris.

And, the vast majority still felt solidly in their bones, without serious thought, in the days of the Revolution and the decades to follow, that that simply would mean adult white males.

Today, few would argue that mistreatment or exploitation of those who – due to circumstance of birth or whatever – lack the resources of others, by making them inescapably abject servants and menial workers, is justified or just. All humans, we now (most of us) intuit, are intrinsically worthy of freedom. And, our contention, amazingly, is not even with flesh and blood, but with presumptuous corporations.

Additionally, we know if we but think, that no bloodlines should merit elevation above others – something, no doubt, prominent in the minds of the Founders. So, would marshal deeds or service perhaps qualify one for citizenship, such as fighting for liberty for all in the Revolution?

Actually, no. Tolerance and magnanimity were still not the order of the day when it came to racial or ethnic differences from the standard of colonial, or recently-colonial, Anglo-Aryan North America, even in the days of the reputedly large-spirited Revolution and its storied state-building aftermath.

But, curiously, on the one hand, Jefferson's personal ample experiences with people of black African origin held in captivity convinced him that individuals of that race possessed limited mental capacity compared to white Europeans.

And yet, Jefferson ventured the opinion that Native Americans had an unfulfilled capacity for intellectual expression and development equal to that of whites, even though it might take additional centuries for that potential to manifest. While his basis for such a judgment is unclear, it would seem to leave the door open, despite his insistence to the contrary, that such a result, if valid, could be more due to nurture and experience than to inherent nature.[17]

At least some of the American Indian tribes, and factions within others, were reputedly warlike by nature and preference, at least at certain times, and had been for centuries. There was no denying that. But, even so, much of the deadly – spilling into genocidal – violence of the colonial period was, as we have glimpsed already, prompted by what the majority of us today might consider heinous, or to put it more mildly, uncivil and aggressive actions by European settlers, who were inarguably the continent's invaders in a larger sense.

During the gigantic pre-Revolutionary conflict that ignited the whole colonial world during the period of the Seven Years' War (or "French and Indian War") between 1754 and 1766, the most famous and popular military leader in America was British General Lord Jeffrey Amherst.

---

[17] Ibid., p. 137.

As sterling as his reputation then was, though, it was darkened for all time by one particular tactic he sanctioned against the forces of the Ottawa Chief Pontiac, who were, in 1763, laying siege to Fort Pitt, the site of modern Pittsburgh.

As told by historian Carl Waldman: "Captain Simeon Ecuyer had bought time by sending smallpox-infected blankets and handkerchiefs to the Indians surrounding the fort – an early example of biological warfare – which started an epidemic among them. Amherst himself had encouraged this tactic in a letter to Ecuyer." Actually, two separate existing letters from Amherst to Ecuyer, dated July 13 and July 16, 1763, seem to clearly substantiate the claim.[18]

Historian Francis Parkman (1886) drew the same conclusion from a different source, apparently no longer existing. And, reportedly, there were still more communications to the same effect.

On the other hand, Lord Amherst's tactic, certain to indiscriminately and lavishly spread death, is perhaps a harbinger of more widespread colonial American attitudes we don't like to acknowledge in our ancestors. By contrast, this same General Amherst displayed praiseworthy "kindness" to French civilians in the areas traversed during the war. "He had a warm sympathy for the countryside, an interest in people and the way they lived."[19]

Indians, to the contrary, were regarded as fiends or brutes, even though aroused to fury by mistreatment or bullying, and were spoken of openly and commonly as "savages".

Unlike the French, who tended to settle mainly in their own separate colonial realm, at least until the 1760s, settlers in that century from other European nations came and settled mainly in the English colonies, but mostly somewhere off by themselves, in areas not yet well-settled. The Scots-Irish settled in the backcountry of the middle and southern colonies, and the sectarian Germans (the so-called "Pennsylvania Dutch"), in central Pennsylvania and a few in colonies nearby.

The real Dutch, meanwhile, still held onto their farms on Long Island and in the Hudson Valley, with some Huguenot (French Protestant) settlements in the Carolinas. There were many Catholic colonists in Maryland. Elsewhere, the settlers, even in the areas that mainly attracted non-English contingents, were rarely other than Protestant in makeup, of one variety or another.

---

[18] Carl Waldman, *Atlas of the North American Indian,* (New York Facts on File, 1985), p. 108.
[19] Louis Henry Gates, op. cit., p. 44 ff.

The British background people were much preferred. And, even among them, some communities (such as the Germantown Quakers, as already mentioned) exhibited odd political notions, such as anti-slavery. The Scots-Irish in the raw, new country above the fall line, far from tidewater, often felt compelled to separate from the more aristocratic plantation-owners on the southern lowland, so wide were the differences between them.

Women were nowhere considered remotely suited for political rights or participation as yet (except, for awhile in New Jersey, where propertied widows might perhaps be permitted to exercise their husbands' voting rights, by an oversight in the law – which was vaguely-worded, and rescinded in 1801).

But not even free blacks, even if they had served honorably in the military – as had the freed slave Abijah Prince of New England, a veteran of the French and Indian War – were given the right to vote. Unwelcome, as a free black man, Mr. Prince kept getting run out of country neighborhoods by bigoted neighbors, along with his strong-minded wife Lucy Terry. And he never did manage to receive proper attention for his rightful claim to a veteran's pension.[20]

The gamut customarily ran only between hostility and simple indifference to "others" as human beings. What passed for justice depended upon regard, and regard was still, even at the end of colonial times, conceded rarely and stintingly by the small inner circle of those who counted. Others must wait.

---

[20] Gretchen Holdbrook Gerzina, *Mr. And Mrs. Prince, How an Extraordinary Eighteenth-Century Family Moved Out of Slavery and Into Legend*, (New York: Harper-Collins, 2008).

Part 3 – The Revolutionary Generation –
1776 to 1800

The apparent "about-face" *change* in perspective that resulted in the formation of America's challenging, heartfelt *creed* in the truly *revolutionary* generation of its independence seems at first glance to have come out of nowhere. But, in fact, that about-turn – as extraordinary and surprising as it may seem – was *never close* to echoing an *actual change of sentiment* to any great degree regarding the matters at hand across the whole nation and across time.

People everywhere have admired the sentiments that are collected as the tenets of our Revolutionary founding and defining *creed*. Their very precepts are echoed at times in the hearts of almost everyone, *everywhere*. Those sharply worded sentiments have stirred many millions of Americans to deep pride, and continue to do so.

The supreme challenge embodied by America's creed exists, and her people have gloried in its meaning and adopted it as a sort of *idealized* national identity, a sort of fantastical measuring stick, pleasantly imagining that it does define us and separate us from other nations.

However, they haven't, in most instances and respects, stirred Americans individually to personally put those considerations *into effect* in guiding their own actions and thoughts or judging the acts of others – at least, not yet. Acceptance of the creed, to the point of *personification*, still awaits the nation at large.

And, thus ever unguided, we endlessly fall prey – easily and thoughtlessly – to our own (and our misguided leaders') *very worst* attitudes and instincts.

An amazing thing about our almost-subliminal national creed is that it's been *subscribed to* readily since our nation's start as an almost-magical set of propositions by perhaps upwards of 95% of us, because we have been infused with it since the cradle. Yet it doesn't really guide us in our decisions and lifestyles.

This has been the case from the start, even while all of our professed creed's tenets have tended to virtually *reverse* the prevalent conventional wisdom and practice and commonly held preferences throughout the colonies and forming nation up to the time of their promulgation. The actual sentiments that our *creed* set into words appeared suddenly, more-or-less complete (though not necessarily in completed *form*) during the decade of the 1770s.

The reason the *creed*'s handful of (five) remarkable tenets – *popular control of the government, freedom of citizens from government control, all men standing equal before the state, liberty and justice for all, and personal and national independence* – stuck and survived is that they didn't descend to inhabit and distinguish the American mind as they did in a vacuum.

Rather, they resulted from the fact that America's ruling class – the rich and wellborn who had always set the tone – formulated them. Those prominent men suffered the stunning and, for them, novel experience at the start of the ferment that led to the Revolution of degradation and humiliation as petitioners and claimants of rights. Their abusers were a particular class – their "betters" in Britain – who treated *them*, most unfamiliarly to them, as unworthy and low rabble.

From that novel perspective, they embraced the *vision of empowerment as human beings* that would set them and (incidentally and magnanimously) *any* white, male American in their predicament, *free* – a vision that could be used to guarantee and consolidate that freedom.

The problem was that the government that had been designed by them to put in operation and protect *that* promised envisioned and cherished freedom *for all* (at least eventually) was to be operationalized not by angels, but by the very men who had always operated on meaner and lower shared principles rather than the opposite.

And so, the very principles of the fine creed that all of us sincerely *believe* in (at least, in our own way) still loom before us, only partially fulfilled, and some really not at all. It is no wonder the whole thoughtful world admires and yearns for those very – eloquently-stated – principles while our own reputations as a nation fluctuate and often, especially of late, unadornedly fall.

In the rest of this book, I will seek to document the above conclusion as clearly as I can, to see what we have done right, once we had our revolutionary *creed* for direction, and what we have done that has abrogated and all too often applied a brake, ruinously over time, to our vaunted contract of trust and good to one another.

The million tragic digressions, I will show, have generally originated in dangerous intentions and ventures of purely self or factional aggrandizement, doing massive, "un-American" violence to the principles promoting liberty *for all*.

If it is objected that I am not well suited in all cases to render such a verdict (as even-handed as I may profess to be), I'll defer. The reader will have the approximate template in hand, and is welcome to render her or his own verdict as to what may constitute *creedal* – as opposed to *anti-creedal* and destructive – thrusts of action in our national history.

The sustained military effort *called* the American Revolution resolved on the ground the immediate crisis of identity, sovereignty, and thwarted will that the radical vision set forth in what I'm identifying as America's five-part creed. And the ideas embodied there became the *social compact* that bonded the erstwhile Colonies into a distinct and vibrant nation.

But, at the point of victory in the war that ushered the United States of America into the world, the custodians of the new, broadly uplifting vision had only won the right to establish a *government* to try to embody and keep that vision – once the society had purged from its midst the outstanding elements that stood opposed and would have denied as much.

The American *experiment,* as it's now called, was launched specifically to test that vision, which was put beneficially into practice over the long haul. The Constitution and the government it inaugurated did not comprise an *end*, but were the machinery designed to enable *realization* of America's founding creedal vision. The long odds, so often remarked, overcome to prevail in the war actually *underestimate* how unlikely it was that the principles set forth should become durably established throughout the vast stretches of country best suited *on earth* to support and defend them. The question then became, what has happened over the decades and centuries as new generations and newcomers appeared and a *raft* of events intervened?

The war itself was won less by logistics, applied resources, and superior strategy, than by happenstance, help, and sheer pluck and endurance. The happy results were two. One was victory and freedom to organize the aftermath in the midst of the financial ruin that the cruel and trying war had brought. The other was a certain vital cohesion and sharing in the patriotic vision of those who endured in the cause to the end.

The actual magnanimity and faithfulness of those prevailing among the "Founding Fathers" in setting up their devised system of governance is frequently questioned by those who see the Constitution of 1787, even with the Bill of Rights added, as favoring the rich and well-born. But, the tenets of the *creed* itself are still there for all to see; and most indeed *do* claim its principles as their own, as they understand them – many with patriotic fervor. Even today those principles are almost *universally* loved. They serve as a source of admiration and pride in a country unrivaled worldwide.

But, such is a mixed blessing. There is a stubborn tendency of so very many Americans to *confuse* the nearly universally-acclaimed, much-emulated tenets of this idealistic national *creed* with the *reality* of our actions. More often than not, the actions of our officials and potent non-officials representing us are unworthy, even shameful. And our off-hand tendency to conflate the two leads to more than one of our most unpopular, unattractive, least-helpful, and most wrongheaded characteristics: *narcissism, arrogance, and exceptionalism.* Fortunately, not all citizens share these traits.

The tendency, in particular, is to believe in *American exceptionalism* – that America is an exception to the rule and has the right to be judged by different standards of conduct from other nations. The hypocrisy and injustice that result are truly *unctuous* for all who don't thus believe, for those who *do* believe in being a reliably good, fair, and caring neighbor, even self-correcting.

Hence, Americans who genuinely embrace the revolutionary creed would demand that our defense forces be used not as an *offense*, but with us living by – even *exceeding* – the standards we hope to observe and to be observed *in us* by others. And, above all, those who *don't* subscribe to the doctrine of "*American exceptionalism*," placing our nation and our lives naturally on a higher level from others', insist in effect *as one* that we strive to bring our actions fully into line with the high-flown rhetoric of our professed creed, which our propaganda claims we represent.

We believe that those representing us who *oppose* that result in any respect ought to be seen as *counterproductive* and *unworthy* of our trust, or of their role representing us. For, only then can our distinguishing national principles survive and flourish and redeem our good name. I'll have more to say on this idea later.

As a complex legal instrument designed for its uniquely lofty purpose, the Constitution of the United States is not perfect. Its provisions – celebrated at least in precept today – were *themselves* the results of political bargains and compromises struck to insure the document's passage by the convention. Subsequent ratification by the states – *nine* being requisite for adoption – was opposed by a host of objecting interests.

Today, even groups opposed to federal government power almost invariably uphold the Constitution as *their* document of limited government, if only its provisions were understood and respected.

Ironically, the opponents of strong central government back in the day, the Anti-Federalists, were *opposed* to the Constitution's very adoption, on a number of counts that we hear today from the mouths of some of the Constitution's fiercest *advocates*. Chief among the criticisms of the document voiced by the Anti-Federalists prior to its ratification by the states, were the following:

1. The omission of a "bill of rights" (*quickly remedied*),

2. The consolidationist/nationalist character of the new government,

3. The charge of aristocracy,

4. Concerns about taxation (*sound familiar?*),

5. Misgivings about the creation of a standing army.[21]

It was generally presumed during and in the wake of the Revolutionary War that the country, if successful, would assume the character of a more-or-less loose confederation of sovereign states, with the central government little more than a weak organ of coordination and the bulk of power resting in the separate states.

The problem with that sort of government, operative under our original constitution, the Articles of Confederation, was that the universal problems of the collapsed currency, wartime debt, and even the a few others that cried out for central control – such as handling the posts and the navy – could not be addressed without direct taxation.

The states had unmanageable debts and obligations of their own, and various piecemeal objections preventing them from contributing adequately to a central kitty, as directed by the Articles. The 1787 convention to modify the pact found it expedient to design a much stronger central authority – although *not* with the blessing of all those demanding state sovereignty and loose affiliation.

Some of the latter included men who controlled strong power bases within their respective states.

And some simply wanted to avoid paying taxes to *anyone*, especially those for the benefit of people in other economic classes and living elsewhere. A strong consensus in the "national interest" costing them money – regardless of its touted benefits to them – was the *last* thing they wanted, just like the "small government" interests today. (The term *"weak government"* doesn't seem to be much in vogue any longer, since such frequently *do* demand a strong military and police power, at least *ostensibly* to protect them).

The Federalist, or pro-Constitutional, view simply garnered more support in the spirited campaigns leading up to ratification in votes by legislature of each state, and so the proposition became reality in 1789.

Besides America's *creed* and a common attachment to the land, one other factor that unified at least the effectual white community of post-revolutionary America was a growing personal reverence for George Washington, the one solid individual thought most responsible for America's release from what was then regarded as its British bondage.

America's main grievance was more psychological than actual: the American large owner and professional class's unaccustomed feelings of

---

[21] Saul Cornell, *The Other Founders*, (Chapel Hill: Univ. of North Carolina Press, 1999), p. 28.

exploitation and humiliation, leading to stinging disillusionment experienced at the hands of petty and belittling British officials and financial creditors.

The community leaders, best exemplified by General Washington, were able to generalize the resentment and calls for rebellion, and thus gain the needed support, by citing unwarranted *taxes* imposed on staples, like salt and tea, that the poor in particular depended on. (The *Stamp Act*, conversely, predominantly affected the rich by imposing taxes on legal papers and documents.) The promise of the new government, to be led by everyone's hero, Washington, was that it would be *everyone's* government, representing and accountable at the next election – accountable, directly or indirectly, to everyone.

                              *   *   *

President Washington's presumed views on *women* and their place – as home and (at times) estate administrators – but considered inappropriate for political participation, were conventional. His private views on *slavery* may actually have veered to opposition and disapproval (though he continued to hold and direct slaves to the end of his life).

But, owing to his unfortunate involvements early in life with vengeful red men on the military frontier, he did not take kindly to American Indians, and mostly tried to see that their villages were removed in advance from the path of civilized road builders and settlers.

This attitude and attendant widespread action are manifest both in Washington's extensive western campaign during the Revolution, and in the grim wars of removal he sanctioned throughout the Northwest frontier during his eight years in the presidency.[22]

Indeed, no quarter was given the Indian, and the serious start of Indian removal ahead of the settlers' plough was to besmirch the next several decades and involve atrocities regularly against the Constitution's restive charges, the tenants of the government. This harsh, uncompromising and unrelenting aspect of American life started in full operation under President Washington's tenure.

But this stance, as seemingly cruel as it is, should not come as a surprise. For, such still reflected the *prevalent attitude* of the new nation, especially

---

[22] For a documented account of the murderous and shameful Coshocton campaign of extermination conducted in Ohio County, in what is now West Virginia, on orders of General Washington in 1781 (just one regrettable example among many), see Barbara Ann Mann, <u>George Washington's War on Native America</u>, (Westport, CT: Praeger, 2005), p. 137 ff. The Northwest Alliance (Indians) held off the encroaching U.S. military in 1791-92, but were overwhelmed and pushed back at Fallen Timbers in 1794.

along the frontier, and was not to be even recognized as a contradiction, due to the mentality then common to almost – but not *absolutely* – all.

Moravian missionary John Heckewelder noted with wonder and horror, based on his experience on the frontier between 1740 and 1808, that pioneer settlers he knew fervently insisted to him that to kill an Indian was the same as killing a bear or buffalo.[23]

One of the main objections of the Anti- Federalists, who opposed a centralized system of government, was that such would – with its ability to tax – establish a standing army, which would be a menace to the people's liberty. Ironically, a chain of events in rural western Massachusetts known as Shay's Rebellion, on the contrary, convinced many of the need for a standing army to deal with insurgency.

In a nutshell, Shays's Rebellion involved subsistence farmers who, falling into debt due to post-wartime hardship and in danger of losing their lands to creditors, banded together to shut down the courts that were rendering the adverse judgments.

In the end, the wealthy creditors in Boston hired an army of mercenaries to go and beat down the rebels. But, as it happened, only a landslide election of candidates for posts strongly disfavoring their position persuaded them in the end to stand down, in June 1787, while the Constitutional Convention was assembling in Philadelphia.

The next serious insurrection testing or featuring central governmental power – by then already in place – occurred in Pennsylvania and adjoining states in 1798. This was the Whiskey Rebellion, involving farmers upset by perverse markets and prices. Although out of office for more than a year, now ex-President General Washington was persuaded to come back and ride convincingly at the head of a regiment dispatched to enforce the law, completing the point for many that no combination or special interest could stand in opposition to the national interest because there was now ample means of enforcement.[24]

But, on the other hand, the government must not be permitted to overstep its constitutional bounds and repress the people or infringe their guaranteed rights and liberties, either. This was what happened when Washington's less-acclaimed successor, John Adams – tired of being pilloried in the press and on the stump, and perhaps a victim of bad advice – enacted the Alien and

---

[23] See John Heckewelder, *Travels of John Heckewelder in Frontier America*, (Paul A.W. Wallace, ed., Pittsburgh: Univ. of Pittsburgh Press, 1958), p. 158 ff.

[24] David P. Szatmary, *Shay's Rebellion, The Making of an Agrarian Insurrection*, (Amherst, MA: Univ. of Massachusetts Press, 1984); Thomas P. Slaughter, *The Whiskey Rebellion: Frontier Epilogue to the American Revolution*, (New York: Oxford, 1988).

Sedition laws of 1798, which made insightful criticism of the chief executive and administration a crime. The laws, which trampled established constitutional rights, did nothing to improve Mr. Adams's re-electability, and, of course, were repealed at the beginning of Mr. Jefferson's administration.

Regarding the observance of America's *creed*, John Adams was certainly a mixed bag. On the eve of the Revolution, his bold and successful defense of the British officer accused of assault and murder in connection with the Boston Massacre had assuredly struck a blow in favor of the proposition of justice for all, at some cost to Adams' political aspirations.

The *federal* system of government established by the Constitution (characterized by different levels of authority, a separation of powers, checks and balances, and yet a *central* government with its own means, independent of state and local control) was not the *highly*-centralized and powerful *nationalist* government that the men who later made up the Federalist Party wanted and continued to fight for.

The early Federalist Party, led by Alexander Hamilton, ineligible for the presidency himself (probably *deliberately rendered so* by a provision inserted in the Constitution) due to being born on Nevis in the West Indies, nevertheless essentially choreographed the first two presidencies, those of Washington and Adams.

Washington declared his party preference reluctantly, because he believed in no parties or factions and so, in a sense, was neutral. And, to his credit, he forged an administration whose leading members came from both of the emerging sides.

Adams sought, at least ostensibly, to continue Washington's precedent in this regard, keeping Hamilton on as his treasury secretary and serving – *though not by choice* – with Jefferson, a leader of the opposition so-called "Republican" faction or party, as his vice president.

Hamilton won a signal victory within the second administration by getting Adams to appoint his protégé, the Federalist John Marshall, as the nation's fourth (and first consequential) Chief Justice of the Supreme Court, for the purpose of subverting and overturning in practice what Hamilton called the "frail and worthless fabric" of the Constitution through judicial decisions.

An ensuing decision was that of the bench upholding repeatedly the *anti-free speech* 1798 Sedition Act, allowing prosecution of Republicans for criticizing the Federalist president, quite obviously violating the Constitution's Bill of Rights.

The Supreme Court also approved the establishment –seemingly *expressly forbidden* by the Constitution – of Hamilton's great pet project, the federally-chartered Bank of the United States, to privately custodian the government's deposits and assume illegitimately the currency-emitting monopoly assigned to Congress.

Although clearly *not* authorized as such in the Constitution, the first private *Bank of the United States* was established by Hamilton as the federal depository and issuer of currency, based on what he referred to, in all seriousness, as *"implied rights,"* a category encompassing those provisions he *wished* had been included in the Constitution, but weren't.[25]

Likewise, President Adams's *last official act*, hours before sullenly vacating the capital ahead of his Republican successor Jefferson in 1801, was to appoint a whole list of Federalist judges to the various courts in order to stymie the acts of the popularly preferred new administration.

It appears plausible that the Supreme Court precedent most relied upon down to the present to justify a private venture co-opting Congress's clear mandate with regard to currency emission is Hamilton's formulation, stamped approvingly by the Marshall Court.

Jefferson favored a healthy central government (a preference he signaled by supporting adoption of the Constitution, written while he served diplomatically in Europe). But he insisted the government be no more extensive or powerful than necessary to achieve what had been lacking under the Articles of Confederation. Hamilton, by contrast, wanted a grand government run by (and of course benefiting) a splendid wealthy class, with impressive subsidies, high taxation and private control over the currency and the nation's fiscal matters.

Serious Hamilton scholars impute that Hamilton wanted the government to completely control the economy, while Jefferson favored minimal regulation.[26]

Of course it needs to be kept in mind that, in Jefferson's day, such corporate interests that existed had not yet concentrated anything anywhere near the degree of power, positive or negative, to impact the lives of citizens and the nation as we experience today.

Thus, Jefferson's often-claimed patronage of measures and programs restrictive of government economic interference and involvement ought to be carried only so far. Also, it should be noted that, throughout the colonial period and into the national, the stated and actual purpose of governing bodies for granting corporate charters was always *"public use"* or in other words,

---

[25] See Thomas DiLorenzo, <u>Hamilton's Curse, How Jefferson's Arch Enemy Betrayed the American Revolution and What it Means for Americans Today</u>, (Boston: Three Rivers, 2009), p. 26 ff.
[26] For instance, see Thomas DiLorenzo, op. cit., p. 99 ff.

"deep public import," not, as now, the enrichment of investors, no questions asked.[27]

But, Hamilton's bald, unbalanced *favoritism* of wealthy business interests, which long continued as an alternative position, starkly violated the_ national creed, and so became a minority position in the early republic, by rather obviously benefitting a small, self-interested and capable segment of the population at the expense of the rest.

Hamilton, who never uttered a recorded word against slavery, was himself, originally via his wife's family's Hudson Valley estate, the owner of a number of house slaves, who were considered status symbols in late 1700s New York.[28]

Another minority that attempted at times to co-opt the course of national affairs to conform to *its own* preferences and standards and jettison majority sentiment and intent consisted of those who couched their citizenship in the *nation* within more-pervasive sectarian religious precepts and loyalties. Preachers and religious leaders all over the land, back in 1800, inveighed, issued tracts and pamphlets, and filled the papers with letters and treatises warning each and all to avoid electing Thomas Jefferson, a known *deist*, and assumed an atheist, as president, or face the wrath of God. (Ironically, there are "conservative" Christian writers today who are raking through old letters and quotes of the long-dead trying to prove that this same problematical man Jefferson had actually been a devout Christian!)[29]

Thomas Paine, the author of (*among others*) the singularly supremely persuasive patriotic pamphlet <u>Common Sense</u>, the great journalist and propagandist of the Revolution, whom the great Sedition Law dissenter Matthew Lyon proclaimed "the one to whom this nation owes the most for its independence," returned to America in 1802 at the invitation of a grateful President Jefferson.

Over the next few years, which brought him rapidly declining health and ultimately death, he nevertheless faced hatred and mobbing from professing *Christians* who reviled him because, in his celebrated and much-reviled book <u>The Age of Reason</u>, he had expressed *doubt* concerning the origin of their religious faith.

In his last, brutally hard years, Paine suffered the most from the cold indifference of his countrymen, including the denial by Federalists in

---

[27] See Andrew McFarland Davis, <u>*Corporations in the Day of the Colony*</u>, (Colonial Society of Massachusetts, 1894), p. 33.

[28] DiLorenzo, op. cit., p. 10.

[29] See Chris Rodda, <u>*Liars for Jesus, The Religious Right's Alternative Version of American History*</u>, (Charleston, SC: BookSurge, 2006), p. 357 ff.

Congress of his request for desperately needed *simple back wages* for service on a long-ago diplomatic mission in which he had taken part. He died a pauper, his rent paid by a friend.[30]

Mercy Otis Warren, a sharp-penned Massachusetts female Anti-Federalist, wrote an acclaimed three-volume history of the American Revolution (1805), plus a variety of other politically-tinged poems, plays, and essays that drew high praise not only from *Jefferson*, but also from the Federalist Washington and ultimately from Adams, whose role the lady disparaged in her outspoken chronicle.[31] Her acceptance proved that *excellence could ply its way*, regardless of gender. In addition, her success lit the way for countless worthy successes to come by *other* members of America's oppressed, unequal "under-class" segments in the unimaginably radical century on the horizon. Indeed, it appeared then that America's already deep-seated school-mantra of a *national creed* was steadily advancing toward personification one fine day.

---

[30] Jack Fruchtman, *Thomas Paine, Apostle of Freedom*, (New York: Four Walls, Eight Windows, 1994), p. 415 ff.

[31] See Nancy Rubin Stuart, *Mercy Otis Warren, Muse of the Revolution*, (Boston: Beacon Press, 2009).

Part 4 – Breaking the Bounds
& Picking up Steam –
1800 to 1820s

America's successful War of Independence and the launching of the new government meant to secure the ideals of the American Revolution (in distilled form, America's *creed*) were the biggest occurrences of the previous generation. In like fashion, the thrust of the *westward movement*, scattering the rapid growth in the new nation's population and its by-now standard pattern of settlement out across the land beyond the Appalachians, following closely behind the removal of the native inhabitants, was the predominant theme of the first young generation of the nineteenth century.

Hamilton and the partisan Federalists had been less than enthusiastic about easing the way to expansion of the country's ecumene westward, not wanting to dissipate the economic engine by spreading it too thin and too far. They wanted to maintain strict control and the benefit of westward expansion for eastern business interests through federal grants of vast tracts to land companies to disburse for profit and the public purse.

Jefferson and his partisans had intended early on to distribute benefits widely by making farm sites and development lots easily and cheaply available directly to average citizens and, in the process, granting access to equalizing public education.[32]

Their instrument for doing these two things was a measure Thomas Jefferson was originally commissioned by the Continental Congress under the Articles of Confederation to provide. His Northwest Ordinance of 1784, revised in 1787, provided a basis for easily and in regular fashion distributing land and providing self-government for the vast Territory Northwest of the River Ohio. This systemization introduced the uniform quadrilateral land survey to public lands distribution. Starting at a baseline on the Pennsylvania-Ohio border and the Mason-Dixon line and moving westward to the banks of the Mississippi, the far limit of lands ceded by the British in the 1783 Treaty of Paris. In addition, the inexpensive sale of the public lands to settlers

---

[32] The grant-receiving and –dispersing land company middlemen in Federalist western settlement schemes were equivalent to today's health insurance companies in less than simple and direct modern health care schemes devised "to reduce the role of government" – superfluous, substantially raised the cost, and benefitted only them.

reserved the proceeds from one section per township to provide basic schooling for all.[33]

The gigantic territory newly open, bit by bit, to settlers was – as its population increased and spread – to be divided into new states equal to the old, according to Constitutional mandate. Further, quadrilateral division into counties and townships was slated for each new area in turn, with ordinances codified and administered by their enfranchised citizens, i.e. *resident free white males.*

In the third year of Jefferson's first term in the presidency, opportunity arose to expand the benefits of the great system just beginning to take large-scale practical effect. The acquisition of Louisiana would permit extension of the same system and benefits almost unimaginably farther westward, to the crest of the Rocky Mountains, and add, for the first time, an invaluable American port on the Gulf.

In fact, the demographically empty Louisiana Territory, acquired from France for mere pennies per acre, doubled overnight the country's size and made it a hemispheric power.

And Ohio, the first new northwest state, was admitted to the union the same fateful year as the acquisition, 1803.

Louisiana's acquisition by purchase in 1803, legalists were quick to point out, wasn't strictly authorized by *anything* in the Constitution. (Perhaps to *"promote the common defense"* by enriching the country?)[34] However, it certainly *did* serve to forward the extension (at least selectively) of America's *creed*, by fostering availability of equal (to a certain extent) opportunities, seemingly, for generations of future agrarians and townspeople. The Lewis and Clark expedition, soon to follow, served to reveal and showcase the annexed mega-tract's splendiferous worth.

The westward extension of slavery was authorized south of the River Ohio (made hugely more practical in the western regions of the South by the 1793 invention of the cotton gin). But slavery was not legalized north of the Ohio. And, in other ways, the inexorable, lightning-fast, at-all-costs thrust of settlement west exacted a horrific toll on the native population. The precipitate decisions involved permitted rapid handing of the new lands – open, free, and immediately, to an onrushing tide of new settlers.

---

[33] Northwest Territory Celebration Commission, History of the Ordinance of 1787 and the Old Northwest Territory, (Marietta, OH: 1937).

[34] Henry Adams later wrote objecting that President Jefferson had thus "dealt a fatal wound to 'strict construction'". See Henry Adams, *The Administrations of Thomas Jefferson*, (1903, NY: Library of America, 1986), p. 343; David N. Mayer, *The Constitutional Thought of Thomas Jefferson*, (Univ. Press of Virginia, 1994), p. 244.

The effect was to cast the tenets of America's revolutionary creed clashing like so many boulders in the gears of America's destiny. And the forbidding, crucial heart of hearts of that creed – *human equality* – was crushed and cast aside.

Upon taking office, Jefferson inherited America's already then ongoing mortal conflict with Muslim nations, in the form of persistent attacks on Mediterranean shipping by Barbary Coast pirates. Britain and France were also plagued and paid annual "tributes" (bribes) to the Barbary States to keep these pests at bay. The fledgling U.S. had earlier done the same, but still lost hundreds of seamen to impressed enslavement in the process.

But Jefferson resolved to put a stop to all that by sending an armada to block the port of Tripoli, the continued harasser after treaties had been concluded with the other offending states.

Jefferson's blockade failed, though, because the port of Tripoli proved too small and shallow to accommodate the vessels he sent. Then, sorely perturbed, he dispatched a force of mercenaries on a long march across the desert to *blow up* the key American vessel stranded at Tripoli to keep it out of the pirates' hands. Terms of peace were hastily concluded, bringing the affair to an end, even while the Federalists carped that Jefferson had not gone to war because he was a wimp!

In fact, Jefferson and his closest compatriot, Madison, much preferred the use of economic sanctions (which, when applied, reduced the flow of American trade) to war. For that, they argued, was the tool of monarchies.[35]

Jefferson likewise sought to deal firmly with the Indian nations occupying much of the old, still sparsely settled Northwest as well as valuable lands for agriculture beyond the southern frontier.

But here, the preferred tools were treaties and effective trade by licensed agents. President Jefferson had the developed and "civilized" portion of the country protected on its far edges by a long line of forts, and commissioned the platoon commanders and agents dispatched there to deal firmly and persuasively with the tribes. The objective, of course, was securing their removal or, in a very few, most favorable instances, their assimilation as farmers.

The intended result was that America's "vacant" spaces were all to become alike, regularly occupied by agricultural inhabitants, vanquishing the savage hunting way of life by absorption or banishment. Thus was the march of civilization to proceed and triumph by extinguishing the old and unfit

---

[35] Gordon Wood, *Empire of Liberty*, (New York: Oxford Univ. Press, 2009), p. 637 ff.

previous ethnicity. And that was the policy that was set in place to continue for generations.[36]

As explained earlier, Slavery wasn't confined to the South. At least the three states of southern New England, as well as New Jersey and New York, had slaves from almost the beginning, though not in large numbers. Of these states, Massachusetts, to its credit, outlawed slavery by decision of its supreme court in the early 1780s. Of the New England states, Rhode Island had the most slaves per capita, with one in fourteen of that state's residents at the start of the Revolution a slave.

It was the settled opinion of New Englanders, as abolitionist sentiment began to grow in opposition to the southern states' preferred form of labor, that what slavery there was in New England was more benign and gentle. And, not surprisingly, when complete emancipation at home was much discussed, New Englanders seriously wondered if slaves might shed their blackness when freed. They commonly talked in terms of not only abolishing slavery, but of abolishing the black man along with it, detracting as he did from a commonly desired New England homogeneity.[37]

But, attitudes toward slavery split families in New England, as they not a few times did in the South. For instance, of two highly successful trading partner brothers from Revolutionary-era Providence, John and Moses Brown, one was, operating on his own, a slave trader; the other was a leading, principled abolitionist. And they fought tooth and nail over it.

Moses, together with others, founded Brown University out of an old prep school known as Baptist College. In 1786, Robert Carter III – grandson of the dynasty-founding Robert "King" Carter of Carter Hall, a leading land-owner and master of five-thousand slaves in northern Virginia – was experiencing moral qualms over keeping so many, in effect, hostage. He sent his two adolescent sons to be educated at Baptist College, thinking that in New England, they at least would be removed from the blighting reality of slavery. Good sentiment; would it were so.[38]

*   *   *

Jefferson, as president, escaped largely peacefully, avoiding serious, compromising war. James Madison, the "Father of the Constitution" and Jefferson's successor, had to all-out fight the British again in his presidency, in an American "just war" of *national defense* if there ever was one. And, in a

---

[36] See Anthony F.C. Wallace, *Jefferson and the Indians, The Tragic Fate of the First Americans*, (Cambridge, MA: Harvard Univ. Press, 1999), p. 206 ff.

[37] Joanne Pope Melish, *Disowning Slavery, Gradual Emancipation and Race in New England, 1780 – 1860*, (Ithaca: Cornell Univ. Press, 1998), pp. iii-xiii, 163 ff.

[38] Charles Rapp Leve, *Sons of Providence*, (New York: Simon & Schuster, 2006).

national nightmare, he got rousted out from an invaded and burned President's House and city of Washington in the process.

America's War of 1812 was something like Wofford College, through some egregious error, having miss-scheduled once to play Ohio State or USC, and, somehow, in an improbable series of about 100 impossible, miraculous plays and hail-Mary's in a row, coming out winning by a point. And now, a generation later, with the iron man, George Washington, no longer your coach, but instead, a scrawny, stubby, mild little drink-of-water nerd from pampered servant-hood named Jemmy Madison.

So, the leviathan super jock-school, having suffered twenty-five merciless years of ridicule from the big boys and the loss of 630 alumni pledges for losing to *Junior*, comes for a rematch and mops up the field with you for three-quarters. Until your third-team quarterback, a skinny, wiry-tough carrot-top smack-talking walk-on Indian-fighter wonder-kid from the canebrake affectionately referred to as "*Andrew*," saunters off the bench and, turning out to be a disguised reincarnation of *Alexander the Great*, astonishes with a spectacular 95-yard lightning strike for the surge-from-behind winning score to save the day and send the unanimous all-forever #1 monster super-champs limping home, astoundingly saving your turf-destroyed field!

Thus, *national independence*, the bottom-line bare-knuckles indispensible element in America's creed, was secured – *so it seemed* – for years ahead.

The United States of America has almost always been absolutely *abysmal* at managing money. The country has failed at this task to the extent that its very independence, a basic creedal factor, has at times been severely compromised.

During the Revolution, the Continental Congress's printing press paper money (the "Continental Dollar") flowed forth like water, understandably for the time, in a vain attempt to cover the expenses of the war – until "*not worth a Continental*" had defined a whole new standard of worthlessness. In an effort to avoid the serious predicament from recurring in the future, the framers of the Constitution – in Article 1, Section 7 – mandated (or attempted to mandate) 1) that *Congress*, acting for the federal government, would exercise a monopoly on the emission of money in the United States, and 2) that, according to the letter of the Constitution, only coinage of *specie* (the precious metals designated, gold and silver) would be acceptable as legal tender.

Reportedly, there was an attempt in the Convention to add three words to the draft text of the article: "and paper currency." But, that attempt was voted down. And furthermore, the states were disqualified from issuing money.

In subsequent years, for reasons that seem unfathomable, in two of these three stipulations or mandates, Congress very early on, and almost ever since, has been guilty of the most *egregious* violations of that clear Constitutional mandate.

Quite simply, not enough *specie* has ever been available to jettison the expedient of paper money, or provide backing for it, regardless of the pitfalls and fraud occasioned by its use, beyond the role of a mere token.

Thomas Paine, who inveighed against paper money in a well-known pamphlet, based on his own bad experiences with the Continental, explained Congress's continued irrational infatuation with it as follows: "The dream of wealth supplied the reality of it; but when the dream vanished, the government did not awake."[39]

On the other hand, two really feeble reasons (or excuses) are commonly cited to explain Congress's (i.e., the federal government's) abandonment of its mandated monopoly on the issuance and effective management of money for the country. One reason or excuse is that Congress did not relish or enjoy the responsibility of keeping the emission of money in its own hands, and the other is that, in 1791, the Secretary of the Treasury, Alexander Hamilton – who did not favor the provision of the Constitution cited – *seduced* Congress into delegating its money-making power and duty to his special creature, the private first Bank of the United States, promising expert and proficient management.

The Bank of the United States was organized approximately on the plan of the Bank of North America, chartered by the Continental Congress near the end of the Revolution. Hamilton persuaded Congress during the first Federalist administration to embrace the Bank as the principal emitter of currency *for it* and the seat of the federal treasury.

His plea was based of the argument, palatable to Federalists, then in the majority, that a great state or empire required a *great and sophisticated central bank*, organized up to world standards. Twenty years later, in 1811, when the first Bank of the United States came up for re-authorization, with its charter due to expire, the Jeffersonian Republicans, *by then* in the majority, not trusting the Bank (and with the formidable Hamilton gone), permitted it to lapse.

Hamilton's ideological successors, such as Henry Clay, revived the scheme in 1816 to help fund the debts of the second war with England. But, the mistake of having done so was revealed to concerned observers two or three years later with the onset of the Panic of 1819, the first severe recession or depression of the U.S. economy.

---

[39] Thomas Paine, *Dissertations on Government, The Affairs of the Bank, and Paper Money*, (Kessinger Publishing, 2009).

As modern analyst Thomas DiLorenzo put it, citing a well-reputed earlier study, "Beginning in the summer of 1818, the Bank of the U.S. precipitated the Panic of 1819 by a series of deflationary moves [which] ... sharply limited and contracted the loans and note issues of the Bank's branches. This in turn forced the state banks to reduce their loans, and the overall monetary contraction 'led to a wave of bankruptcies throughout the country', the real estate bubble burst, as prices overall fell precipitously ... personal bankruptcies abounded..."[40]

So, why was it that Congress, even acting on the basis of common sense, if its members could not summons the propriety to respect the mandate in the Constitution, would permit for even one hour private manipulation and profit-taking from the nation's financial system at the entire public's expense? Indeed, *what could* have induced Congress to even consider doing that – in those days or *now?*

And yet, to the contrary of all common sense, once the deleterious effect of the private central bank on the nation's finances became clear for all the world to see, Congress was quick to let matters *become even worse*, by permitting the *states* to charter currency-emitting banks, too.

Why, then, if Congress farmed out the privilege, couldn't full-service banking, providing loans in the form of printed bank notes (currency), be regarded as just another licensed business? Because the central government, depositing its revenue from tax receipts, had to borrow to pay for any amount needed of what was legally *its own* money at interest, and because the banks, holding a certain amount of genuine wealth in the form of *specie*, could issue it out again and again and again in the form of currency emissions, without anyone becoming the wiser. And collect interest on all of *those* many-fold "emissions" as well.

So, how was it that private banking, thus endowed, compromised the nation's *independence?* Because the government didn't issue its own money under the central bank system, but had to order it at interest. And most of the shareholders who collected payments from interest from the first Bank of the United States were British bankers and their American operatives. Also, the central bank, *its stock mostly held abroad*, profited additionally from supplying the branch and local banks with funds at interest.[41]

The number of note-issuing banks chartered by states, once that practice began, after the chartering of the original Bank of the United States, increased to more than three-hundred over the next seventy-five years, until there was

---

[40] Thomas DiLorenzo, op. cit., p. 68, citing Murray Robards, *The Panic of 1819*, (Auburn, AL: Mises, 2007), p. 19.
[41] See Ellen Hodgson Brown, *Web of Debt*, (Baton Rouge: Third Millennium, 2007), p. 48.

little to distinguish the rampant counterfeiters (*unauthorized* emitters of bank notes) from the state-authorized, but uncontrolled, *legal* emitters. People accepted and spent the ubiquitous counterfeiters' notes, too, because they *assumed* (mistakenly) that they were properly backed up by specie (which the legal emitters' notes weren't, either).[42]

So, the United States' official money supply system was not (and *is not*) appreciably different in its fundamentals from those counterfeiters' and continues to cost the nation unnecessarily, now to the tune of *hundreds of billions* assessed annually to support its purchases of credit and cash. All in blatant disregard of the plain text of the Constitution's Article 1, Section 7, *no matter how it is read.* So, again – *what is it,* pray tell, that so resoundingly trumps the Constitution of the United States for the main actors in our political system?

The first Bank of the United States, understandably not re-chartered in 1811, was re-instated by most of the same politicians, renamed the *Second Bank of the United States* in 1816, ostensibly to assist in financing the just-concluded War of 1812, illustrating the narrow practical distance between disgust and avarice.

The Monroe Doctrine (1823), promulgated by President James Monroe's Secretary of the Treasury, John Quincy Adams, outwardly sought to protect the new, emerging republics of the New World from further invasion by powers from the Old World. The first problem with this was the fact that the protecting English-speaking North American republic lacked the power as yet to enforce much of anything. The second was that, as the United States did grow dramatically in resourcefulness and power in later years, the Monroe Doctrine tended to clear the field of rivals to overweening U.S. interference south of our borders. So, the *actual* meaning of this celebrated pronouncement turned out to be something like the old definition of a "gentleman" – *a man who resolves to protect a lady from everybody but himself.*

In this period, America was, of course, still far from being the industrial and post-industrial colossus it would become. In fact, the decades straddling the turn of the nineteenth century marked the very earliest beginnings of the entry of the United States into the dawning age of the Industrial Revolution.

American industry, powered apart from human or animal exertion, can be said to have had its start with the advent of Slater's Mill at Pawtucket, Rhode Island, in 1793 – a water-powered cotton mill operation. (Its design was essentially the same as for a *horse-powered* mill opened at Beverly, MA in 1787). Cotton and woolen mills proliferated, dotting the southern New

---

[42] Stephen Mihra, *A Nation of Counterfeiters*, (Cambridge, MA: Harvard Univ. Press, 2007), pp. 8, 16.

England countryside by the teens of the new century. And, perhaps not so oddly, when you think about it, the very first industrial workforce, and the earliest pioneers of collective bargaining also, in America were *women* – or rather, New England farm girls, to be precise.

So, New England farmers, whose own back-breaking exertions grew meager crops of often-blasted wheat and ample stones on hard land, and who sent their second, and third, and ninth sons off to harvest fish and whales on the seven seas or west to open up better farms, were now sending their *daughters* to the mill towns. The work of these young girls provided supplementary income, often feathered a dowry, and, most significantly, gladdened the pots of potentially-powerful trade tycoons and ship owners who were the investors and made *them* fatter and happier.

Though there were no industrial regulations and the factories were cold, damp, and dirty, the hours impossibly long, the wages a pittance, and working with the machinery of the day was hazardous and nerve-wracking, the girls liked having something they could do to be *"independent."* And, usually broken and worn-out at a still-tender age, they would frequently come back home to spin and eventually die.

The owners balked at making a woman a supervisor. When the matter of a qualified one came up – *it didn't happen.* The low wage meant high profits for the mills, as they expanded their clientele outward globally and became as rich as Croesus.

Then, after a few years, the female workers were discarded in favor of new immigrants who would work, uncomplainingly, for less. Eventually, the New England mills all closed down as textiles began to be milled closer to the cotton supply. And the farmers, lacking produce, started shipping ice to the Orient. Woman, thus also first began to experience the downside of the American working-class's exclusive equality of that day.[43]

The leading historic role assumed by the U.S. Supreme Court, at the head of the federal government's third, *conceptually* equal branch, was that of ruling in a binding fashion on the constitutionality of laws passed as well as deciding cases sent up on appeal from lower federal courts.

That eventual primary function was only established by the Court under its fourth Chief Justice, John Marshall, as we have seen, a Hamilton accolade and John Adams appointment, in a minor but signally important binding decision in the case of Marbury v. Madison in 1803, which declared the Judiciary Act of 1789 "unconstitutional" – *a first-time designation.*

In Fletcher v. Peck (1810), the Marshall Court further strengthened the sanctity of contracts and excluded the state courts from arbitrarily overturning

---

[43] See William Moran, *The Belles of New England,* (New York: St. Martins, 2002).

the political decisions of state legislatures, siding with the politically-accountable representatives and – perhaps surprisingly from *this* Court – enjoining courts from legislating, in favor of popular control.

In 1819, in the case of Marbury v. Maryland, in the midst of a great financial panic brought about by manipulations of the Second Bank of the United States, just three years after its chartering by Congress, Congress's power to do so was brought into question and decided by the Court. John Marshall, writing the opinion for the unanimous Court, ruled that Congress *did* have that power, and that the state of Maryland, where it was located, had no power to tax it, because it was *federally*-chartered. Thus, the Court decided specifically to the advantage of the exclusive business oligarchy that profited from the Bank.

The Court's again unanimous decision in the case of Gibbon v. Ogden, five years later, likewise affirmed the primacy of charters granted by a federal agency over state charters. This time, the gist involved navigation (defined as "commerce") on an interstate waterway. Thus, again to the dismay of the small-government Jeffersonian Republicans, the power of the federal government was upheld and enhanced.

In Woodward v. Harvard College (1819), contracts even when set in motion and stipulated by a long-dead prior, colonial government, were confirmed to be still fully operative and *unalterable*, in every respect, by currently-existing governments.[44]

The third decade of the now-not-so-new century, a decade of unprecedented grown and change – *as every succeeding decade seemed to turn out to be* – brought the deaths of both Jefferson and John Adams, on the 50th anniversary of America's much-jeopardized independence. This decade brought the *end* of spurned Federalism as an elective political movement, but, paradoxically, the theft of the presidency from the clear enough popular choice, the hero Andrew Jackson. And it brought his vindication at the polls four years later.

Additionally, that decade of the *twenties* brought many more destructive blows for the *creedal* propositions of *all men created equal* and *justice for all*. Was progress being made toward America's self-realization? *Selectively.*

The institution of slavery, the sullied social order primarily ensconced in the South, was beginning with some frequency to split families in that region, even as it did in the North, where some hated it, while others *feared* it more.

By the 1820s, independent-minded Sarah Moore Grimke, daughter of a Charleston, South Carolina slaveholding family, became a grown woman and

---

[44] See Gordon S. Wood, op. cit., pp. 440-442, 455 ff.,465; Peter Irons, *A People's History of the Supreme Court*, pp. 104-107, 112-115, 121, 126-129, 131-134.

moved to Philadelphia, where her lifelong anti-slavery sentiments, which had shocked her parents, *flourished* in more favorable air and soil and she became a superstar abolitionist. With fourteen children and a flock of slaves to oversee, it appears to have been a case of the parents losing control, with dissention brewing ominously among the young already in the solid South.[45]

By the end of that decade, in northwest Georgia, one notch farther down the seaboard, a magic word none had been able to utter aloud and be thought sound a short time before was suddenly on everyone's lips: "Gold!" And the yellow metal had, improbably enough, been found on and around the land held by the best examples there were of Thomas Jefferson's assimilated, culturally-appropriate and peaceful natives, the literate and civilized, small-town and farming, good "citizen" Cherokees.[46] *What next?*

---

[45] See Mark Perry, loc. cit.
[46] See David Williams, *The Georgia Gold Rush, Twenty-Niners, Cherokees, and Gold Fever*, (Columbia: Univ. of South Carolina Press, 1993.

Part 5 – Breaking Sweat – 1830 to 1850s

Ironically perhaps, one would be hard-put to discern the spirit of America's heartfelt *creed* in the outward acts of the third generation of Americans, even while parts of it were being admiringly *pronounced* daily from a million proud lips. Movements, however, were afoot then; venturing boldly, even brazenly in the direction of true equality and justice.

Alexis de Tocqueville, an aristocratic Frenchman, toured and studied the United States close-up in the first presidential term of Andrew Jackson. Then, he published his revealing findings in two book-length installments, in 1835 and 1840, entitled famously, in their English translation, <u>Democracy in America</u>.

Tocqueville described American society, politics and the U.S. economy admiringly and, most would concede, accurately. He noted that market capitalism had a strong foothold in the country and a strong claim on the interests and exertions of nearly all Americans. And Tocqueville wrote, perceptively, that a democratic government needed to remain both "active and powerful"[47] in order to carry out its public purpose: none of the anemic state.

Captivated by the energy and resourcefulness of the America he found, he recorded that "commercial business is there like a vast lottery, by which a small number of men continually lose, but the state is always a gainer."[48] A *gainer*, neither pauper nor weakling.

Many thoughtful Americans of that time, both North and South, assumed that the representatives of those two great regions must have struck a bargain in Philadelphia at the Constitutional Convention more that half a century earlier, to the effect that the interests of the South would predominate and would not be seriously disrupted. It was considered in the South's interest, it was often pointed out, to keep its residents of African origin perpetually in subjugation, and to benefit even legally and electorally as a result. Such was declared, therefore in the *nation's interest*.[49]

In fact, an old New England axiom, widely known, had it that the Constitution had been founded "not on 'Righteousness of God,' but on 'Slavery and Blood.'"[50] At the time the Constitution was promulgated and for

---

[47] Alexis de Tocqueville, <u>Democracy in America</u>, Vol. 2 [1840], (New York: Knopf, 1960), p. 236, 323.

[48] Ibid., p. 236.

[49] Also paramount to the South's strength was the fact that southern cotton came to account for 80% of U.S. exports.

[50] Leonard L. Richards, <u>The Slave Power</u>, (Baton Rouge: LSU Press, 2000), p. 36.

years afterward, it was assumed that the federal government would be forced to resort to a head tax assessed on *individuals*. Accordingly, the South's *3/5 compromise* formula was originally intended to reduce the *tax liability* of southern slaveholders.

Of course, that long-defunct formula, the mere mention of which is considered mildly derogatory, and, at best, fodder for edgy humor to this day, became important – ironically – because it was used to increase the *representation of the southern states* in Congress and the Electoral College in order to protect slavery. And, for generations, that formula in fact prevented the increasingly anti-slavery North from claiming an advantage by effectively controlling either Congress or the presidency. As a consequence, even presidents who hailed from the North necessarily remained acutely conscious of the political support they needed from the South; so, at best, they dithered on slavery.

But, then, there was also the *fugitive slave provision* in the Constitution, as well as the injunction against ending the slave trade, to halt introduction of new stock and reinforce southern slave numbers by importation until 1807.

Either tampering with that particular strain of Constitutional balance, or adding to southern uneasiness regarding suspected northern intent to attack slavery, through manipulation of those and other such matters, was considered *dangerous nationwide* to the overriding objective of maintaining equanimity and, above all, cohesion. So, for many years, to speak of abolition was considered *unspeakably radical* and, for a long time, highly objectionable – as a potentially explosive, self-policed taboo in polite society.

In the meantime although, in the new, expanding Northwest – just as in New England – abolitionism was starting be becoming the new norm, based on irrepressible sentiments of morality. Still, free blacks were seldom welcomed as neighbors, let alone friends. And, even in northern states and localities, where free blacks were at least permitted to live, they were almost universally *restricted* in mobility and other rights and excluded from community affairs.[51]

In some ways, the president at the time was perfectly representative of America. President Jackson was neither a homespun eccentric nor near-imbecile, nor aristocratic planter cynically posing as a democratic champion (as different factions claimed, and their ideological successors still do). Instead, President Jackson was a sincere and tireless champion of the interests of the whole nation, as he understood them, including constitutional

---

[51] See Robert R. Dykstraw, *Bright Radical Star, Black Freedom and White Supremacy on the Hawkeye Frontier*, (Cambridge, MA: Harvard Univ. Press, 1993).

government – which he took as his mandate – and ever standing opposed to the triumph of narrower and destructive interests.

His decidedly flamboyant record of financial action alone attests to that essential truth, but is not commonly understood. His famous, robust "war" against the clearly unconstitutional Bank of the United States climaxed the Bank's second incarnation after being resurrected in 1816, following a five-year hiatus, under the subterfuge of a need for help with expenses following the War of 1812. Jackson's bank war was itself, to a great extent, a war to secure America's independence.

From its original foundation as the first Bank of the United States in 1791, the stock of this controlling, currency-emitting central bank was up to 75% *English*-owned. And the Bank's managers were principally the money managers for these particular foreign owners' American interests.[52]

Jackson's causing the Bank to liquidate *ended* (for that time) the ability of the British banking interests – substantially, our recent colonial masters – to siphon enormous quantities of money paid at interest on loans out of the American economy. (The top British bankers of the day – led by the Bank of England – were closely aligned as well to interlocking bank interests all over continental Europe, headed by the Rothschild family, who had also gained control of British states' finance).

In the course of the 1830s Bank fight, it was divulged that the "retainers" paid by the Bank to members of Congress had smoothed the path for the whole widely distrusted labyrinthine system.[53] The question actually posed then was: could foreign bankers be permitted to finance, control, and draw profits commensurately from America's enormous and rapid development? President Jackson's answer was effective and emphatic.

Having banished the private central bank from the American scene, Jackson was able in short order to oversee the retirement of the plaguing national debt, for the first and only time. Following his hard-won victory over the "monster" Bank, getting the renewal of its charter for another twenty years defeated a couple of years early in Congress, he didn't wait, but removed the funds of the federal treasury at once.

Nicholas Biddle, the Bank's Director, counter-attacked through various measures, openly attempting to wreck and shake the U.S. economy into submission to his will – a flagrant abuse of power that later brought his

---

[52] Karl Erich Born, *International Banking in the 19th and 20th Centuries*, transl. (Warwickshire, UK: Berg, 1983), p. 16.
[53] Even such a well-reputed giant statesman as Daniel Webster inquired about an expected "retainer" from Nicholas Biddle, the head of the Bank, possibly for legal counsel.

indictment. He was it appears, saved from time in prison only by his timely death.

Meanwhile, President Jackson, bolstered by overwhelming re-election to office, continued his deadly-serious campaign, next attacking British financiers' suspected draining of money out of America via voluminous loans for land speculation, which became the leading national sport, engineered though majority ownership in a spate of state and local U.S. banks. Jackson's chosen weapon was the "Specie Circular," issued by presidential order in 1836. This new U.S. law required all land purchases to be in gold or silver. And the action taken *proved dramatically* the President's point by abruptly causing several British banking houses, dependent on siphoning America's money, to fall.[54]

But, Jackson, while preferring specie, was practical enough to realize that coinage alone was not capable of covering all of America's financial needs, as desired by the Constitution's authors.

He pointed out that, although the framers stipulated that only Congress was to have the power to coin money, they obviously didn't intend by that provision to limit Congress to *metals* while relinquishing to banks the power to produce *the rest* of the money supply! Congress's monopoly on the issuance of money he interpreted as *written in stone* – and not to be delegated.

The philosophy that approved of letting super-wealthy conglomerates control the country, even if by illegitimate means, concentrating productivity into their hands and praying for as many crumbs as there are grains of sand on a beach to fall to regular individuals, has been with us always.*

In fact, according to one of our least-known Founding Fathers, John Jay, the nation's first chief justice, writing in 1787, "The people who own the country ought to govern it." Problem is, that's denying the stake that *everyone* has in the outcome.

Early in the 19th century, the states in the North started to develop a variety of industries, while leaders in the South chose to stick to big cash crop agriculture in order to concentrate their investments, using slaves to produce export commodities on a large scale. This simple "colonial"-style of economy was practiced across the South, wherever the landscape and ready access to natural water transport would permit.

---

[54] Murray N. Rothbard, <u>*A History of Money and Banking in the United States*</u>, (Auburn, AL: Ludwig von Mises Institute, 2005), pp. 98-99, explains that the Jackson administration's Specie Circular was not, has often been said, the cause of the Panic of 1837, that being caused by the Bank of England, worried about inflation in the UK, exporting gold and tightening the money supply internationally.

Thus, railroads, when they developed, and other so-called *"internal improvements,"* including canals and turnpikes, came to be much more northern phenomena. And southerners disdained public support for internal improvements, meaning expenses shared across all regions. Projects for internal improvement were greatly resented and resisted by southern leaders, even though the increases in productivity they heralded benefitted the South as well as the North.

In addition, members of Congress from the North favored the imposition of high import tariffs on goods in order to encourage their developing manufactures by protecting them from foreign competition. But the southern members hated tariffs, particularly high tariffs, because they significantly increased the price of everything the South had to import from the North or abroad – *which was practically everything.*

By 1828, southern senators and representatives had gotten so sick of arguing against measures for high tariffs – seriously needed by the North to spur economic growth – that one of them devised a plan. To emphasize their point, one of them (in fact, Senator John C. Calhoun, soon to be Jackson's vice president) introduced a bill that would set tariffs at what he thought would be considered a ridiculously high level – *but garner support in New England for the southerner Jackson.* The conspirators were confident that such a bill would never pass. *But, it did!* And the notorious result came to be called the "Tariff of Abominations," the highest tariff ever passed in the United States.

South Carolina politicians, in particular, both within that state and in Congress, grew desperate thereafter nearly to the point of apoplexy over what they construed as an extreme measure *thrust upon them* by northern votes. The tariff in effect was so extreme, they said, that they questioned its Constitutionality, benefitting, so they argued, one section of the country at such an extreme expense of another section.

Accordingly, they contrived, as a counter-measure, a new doctrine called *"nullification"*. By this doctrine, a state could *"nullify"* (declare invalid or *null*) a federal law within its own boundaries if necessary to protect itself.

For his part, President Jackson, although a southerner, viewed the doctrine of nullification – which was actually invoked in South Carolina – as a grave threat to the integrity of the union. The union of states, he argued, was a compact to benefit Americans in *every* state, meaning that its legally constituted measures could not be opted out of individually.

Vice President Calhoun, responsible in no small part for the doctrine himself, resigned his post and returned to South Caroline to seek re-election to the Senate in order to support it and fight the tariff.

But Jackson, as we have seen, was not to be trifled with on constitutional matters. Ominously, he warned that nullification was treason. And then, he declared that, unless the South Carolinians stood down, the leaders responsible would, accordingly, be hanged.

Not surprisingly, even the fire-eaters stood down and withdrew the measure. And so it was that Andrew Jackson, the nation's seventh president, bloodlessly preserved the union and defended the Constitution – which he had pledged and taken such pains to obey in terms of the nation's finances, and in all other ways.[55]

Perhaps worried more about their own futures, members of Congress, in the meantime, had gotten so alarmed by the seeming impending crisis threatening dissolution of the union that they lowered the tariff somewhat (not *too* much, lest it lose votes for many of them). But their response had little effect until the President's threat and decree registered.

Perhaps as a reward for his efforts for the ordinary citizen, Jackson, the most potent and yet popular of presidents, was fired at twice point- blank in succession by a would-be lone assassin on the White House steps, from *two guns – both of which jammed –* an occurrence calculated at less than a one-in-a-million chance. Inured to frontier justice, the President himself grabbed and severely caned the man.

But then, neither was Jackson, the plainspoken southerner, a total *nationalist* flak, either. And he did not inevitably side with federal authority against the desires of a particular state. His response to complications caused by the *sizable gold discovery* on land occupied by peaceful Cherokee farms and towns in north Georgia being a case in point.

After word had spread about the gold, Georgia quickly took it upon itself to revoke the Indians' previously established rights to the land and declare state control. Encouraged by extreme circumstances, the state even attempted to kick federal *peacekeeping troops* off the land – another seeming provocation. So, which way would the president ultimately tilt?

Jackson, sympathetic by background and lifetime inclination to the desires of the white Georgians, surely dismayed many of his supporters by pursuing

---

[55] See William W. Freehling, *Prelude to Civil War*, (New York: Oxford Univ. Press, 1966). The "Force Bill" was the decree to send troops south to enforce the order. Ironically, the previous threat of disunion had involved the New England states, whose representatives met in Hartford in 1814 to discuss separation because they doubted the U.S. armed forces, such as they were, would be able to defend them from a feared British re-invasion. Thus, they wished not for weaker, but for stronger and more-capable federal power. Ironically, it was Jackson, at New Orleans, who had provided the answer then, too.

still another vigorous response – that of *ramming the Indian Removal Act through Congress.*

The Cherokee, for their part, were sophisticated enough to file suit in court to challenge their removal and seek adequate protection and restoration of their thoroughly legitimate rights. And their petition ended up before the U.S. Supreme Court.

The Court, still led by Chief Justice John Marshall, *found in favor of the Cherokee.* And, President Jackson's infuriating response was: "John Marshall has made his decision; let him enforce it."

The Georgia Cherokee were soon, most lamentably and sadly, on their way down the "Trail of Tears," on the long, grueling march so dolefully remembered, to the Indian Territory (now Oklahoma), a land foreign to them, that was reserved beyond the Mississippi.

And generations of Americans since have judged severely the rough-hewn old soldier president for imposing such a decision, countermanding the Court's.

But, let it be at least considered what the alternative decision on his part would most certainly have meant. To enforce the Cherokees' rights and the Marshall Court's decree would have involved *ordering U.S. troops*, from the South as well as North, to combat the inevitable invasion of gold- and land-seeking Georgians and other Americans.

The first victims of such a conflict, in that time and place, would *inevitably* have been the *Cherokee*, who Andrew Jackson almost certainly saved from annihilation by ordering their removal. *And probably also saved the union again!* Though the price was trashing his own *sterling reputation for fairness and battling for freedom*, he had no real choice.[56]

The even more famous and momentous western analog to the Georgia gold cycle, of course, was the series of precious metal booms launched in the "Far West" by the discovery of gold at Sutter's Mill in newly-acquired California twenty years later.

The great influx of precious metals (or *specie*) thus availed added tremendously to the nation's stock of currency and wealth, financed American industrialization, bolstered American independence, and added immeasurably to the amount of wealth the European banking concerns aspired to garner through somehow re-establishing their machinery to siphon another mega-fortune in American loans. And again, Indians were decimated.

---

[56] See David Williams, op. cit., pp. 31, 38-40. At the same time, Jackson's overall views of non-whites would seem quite dated and inappropriate today.

In the North, a veritable logjam of "stubborn" Indian occupation slowed the opening up of vast tracts of some of the world's most-fertile farmland on both sides of the Mississippi. The blockage was dislodged by superior military force applied against the Sac and Fox confederacy led by Chief Black Hawk later in the 1830s.[57] North and South, the "obstacles" to civilization and democracy were steadily removed.

The Sioux and other Plains tribes were dislodged from their grazing and gold-laden lands farther west a long generation later. The Comanche posed an even more formidable, analogous roadblock to American expansion farther south, a challenging restraint Americans inherited from other long-stymied empires.

Major Ethan Allen Hitchcock, commissioned to investigate the delivery of supplies promised by treaty to the Georgia Cherokee, who were now wards on reservations on the southern plains, filed his report with the government in 1841. In it, he cited rampant "bribery, perjury, and forgery, short weights, issues of spoiled meat and grain, and every conceivable subterfuge employed by designing white men." Then, with the condemnatory truth in hand, the government made the predictable decision *not* to issue Hitchcock's honest report to the public.[58]

Andrew Jackson's immediate successors in the presidency all turned out to be relatively lackluster, in terms of accomplishments and resolution.

The administration of Martin Van Buren of New York, Jackson's close associate and second-term vice president – who succeeded him directly – was thwarted by a dramatic economic downturn, widely blamed then and now on Jackson's policies. But recent studies have tended to vindicate Jackson even in this.[59]

After 1840, the presidency passed among a variety of relatively bland figures, some of them northern, but invariably sharing southern political connections and sympathies, all unwilling to come to grips with the looming slavery issue. No one who was willing could have attracted enough support to attain the White House.

Likewise, the national parties – the Democrats and the new Whigs, baptized as an anti-Jackson party after his two successful but ultimately divisive terms – were shallow alliances of convenience, essentially lacking in core principle, each sporting its own fairly vapid northern and southern wings.

---

[57] Service during the Black Hawk War constituted the sum of Abraham Lincoln's military experience pre-1860.

[58] Carl Waldman, op. cit., p. 226.

[59] See above, under Specie Circular.

But, sharply contrasting with the foregoing, the decade of the 1840s *itself* was a time of roiling cultural ferment, and social activism and movements, unrivaled in that respect for decades to come.

Spiritualism and the perhaps even more arcane Transcendentalism were all the rage. Single-issue third parties were fashionable. The "Great Awakening" of Protestant revivalism hit another peak, featuring huge tent meetings and fiery preaching, and Mormonism started out as a distinctive spinoff.

Abolitionism, remaining a sensitive taboo topic, North and South, through the 1830s, was soon sweeping across the North thereafter, with a brave sprinkling of adherents in Dixie as well.

Black people in those years were openly and deliberately made to feel inferior mentally and in terms of personal worth. David Walker, a free black man and editor of Freedom's Journal, the first American black newspaper, published in New York, wrote in 1829 (early in the Jackson period), "We [black people] of these United States, are the most degraded, wretched, and abject set of beings that ever lived since the world began... and the white Christians of America, who hold us in slavery, (or, more properly speaking, pretenders to Christianity), treat us more cruel and barbarous than any heathen nation did among people whom it had subjugated."[60]

The motives of many marginal or false adherents to the abolitionist cause and northern politicians using the movement or sentiment as a vehicle may not have been pure. But the true believers at the movement's core made it up to blacks for the deceits they suffered by accepting such prominent black figures as Frederick Douglass as exemplary equals and friends, showing what could be.

The Grimke sisters from South Carolina, mentioned earlier, transcended their slaveholder roots to assume positions of leadership in the nationwide movement for abolition. Southern opinion was keenly aware of and duly alarmed by the movement and its searing rhetoric.

The surge for recognition and equality with men for American women was not far behind abolitionism in visibility and organization. But still, the capacity of women for true understanding and expression, somehow remained for the deciders, American males, more a matter of conjecture than certainty – much as for the capacity of non-whites.

Women had been essentially the captives and muses of men in Western Civilization from time immemorial. Progress had been made, but little. Until even a handful of years before, the most capable and fortunate women in

---

[60] Louis Henry Gates, op. cit., p. 58 ff. The dogged insistence of the traditionally oppressive culture on black feeble-mindedness is strongly suggestive of a guilt symptom, perhaps groping, if irrationally, for some justification.

America had been able to rebuke their husbands' basically misogynist attitudes only very mildly.

Abigail Adams, for instance, wrote to John in 1776, upbraiding him with: "I cannot say that I think you are very generous to the ladies; for whilst you are proclaiming peace and goodwill to men, emancipating all nations, you insist upon retaining an absolute power over wives."[61]

The modern women's rights movement in America got its start, according to general consensus, in a meeting of five women, led by Elizabeth Cady Stanton and Lucretia Mott, at Waterloo in upstate New York on July 13, 1848. This discussion over coffee (or tea?) was preliminary to a women's rights convention at nearby Seneca Falls six days later.[62]

Change, inching toward a fulfillment of the glorious promises explicit in America's founding creed, was precociously in the air in that heady decade: a forerunner of the headstrong and sullied unleashing, frightening for many, in the 1960s.

Back in the early 1820s, three hundred Americans, organized by Moses Austin, settled in Spanish Texas – nearly uninhabited, except by the fearsome Comanche – at the behest of the colonial government of pre-independence Mexico. Austin, originally from Connecticut, was a frontier developer in early Missouri. His son, Stephen F. Austin, led the contingent, following Moses Austin's untimely death. Restless, the hardy original settlers protested the decision by the "arbitrary" government of newly-independent Mexico to abolish slavery. Shortly afterward, the Texas colony petitioned for statehood in Mexico. Their request was turned down, and Austin, the emissary to Mexico's president, was jailed for over a year in Mexico City.

In the mid-1830s, the colony formed a provisional government and declared itself a republic. This action brought an invasion by the Mexican army and produced an influx of volunteers, some of them prominent, mostly from the southern U.S., to fight for Texas independence. By 1836, their effort succeeded, and Texas was on its own.

Nine years later, led by the frontier republic's president, its revolutionary hero Sam Houston, and finding itself financially distressed, Texas petitioned for annexation to the U.S. and admission as a state. In 1845, its request was granted, within a month after the death of the annexation effort's great patron, "Old Hickory" – ex-President Jackson.

---

[61] Miriam Gurko, *The Ladies of Seneca Falls, The Birth of the Women's Rights Movement*, (New York: Schocken, 1974), p. 21.

[62] Involved in this movement, too, both as letter-writers and as speakers, were the liberated Grimkes. See Miriam Gurko, op. cit., p. 30 ff.

Mexico, understandably, protested the Americans adding Texas to their empire, and started a skirmish against a provoking force of U.S. troops sent to patrol south of the Nuecos River, long accepted as Texas's southern boundary.

The attack by the Mexicans was nevertheless presented to Congress by President James K. Polk as a pretext for requesting a declaration of war against Mexico. And Congress, a majority of its members eager for further southern expansion, obliged.

Harsh critics, both of the war and the administration's ethics in provoking an incident to launch unnecessary aggression, included Abraham Lincoln. Lincoln, a one-term Whig congressman from Illinois, painstakingly pointed out that the American contingent had been attacked by the Mexicans on Mexican territory. He filed a series of objections in Congress, stating as much, which came to be called *"spot resolutions"* – earning him a derisive nickname, "Spotty Lincoln."

It was also objected by many in the North, especially New Englanders, that the war with Mexico was really a southern offensive war, against a country that could easily be defeated. The observation proved true, on both accounts – even though, as it turned out, for reasons of climate, Texas was the only new slave state secured. But the desire was for more.

A couple of years earlier, with expansion into the Oregon country on the Pacific in prospect, a Whig congressman from Georgia, Robert Toombs, declared revealingly that he didn't "want a foot of Oregon or an acre of any other country – especially without 'niggers'." With Texas and lands of the Southwest in offer, however, arid but technically open to slavery, his designs and other southerners' changed. Vast new territory and another new state, California, were quickly added to the union as a result of the Mexican War. There was talk of adding Cuba as well.

The fact was that, with growing abolitionist sentiment in the North and movement westward advancing rapidly in that quarter, the South felt constrained to add more and more land and new states open to slavery to its domain in order to exercise control over legislation.[63]

The key policy votes in Congress and the key Supreme Court cases of that era (with Roger B. Taney of Maryland – pronounced *"tawney"* – presiding as Chief Justice after 1836) all had to do with the expansion of slavery into new territory. Meanwhile, New Mexico, settled in places for centuries, had to be

---

[63] See Robert H. Wiebe, *The Opening of American Society*, (New York: Knopf, 1984), pp. 358-360.

occupied by U.S. troops until 1851 to maintain civil order and expedite American rule.[64]

Long in retirement, Jefferson had noted in a letter back in 1820, his reaction to Congress's so-called "Missouri Compromise," prohibiting the admission of any new slave states, except for (in the present instance) Missouri, to the north of that new state's southern border. Missouri was paired with Maine, a new, entering free state.

The necessity for this legislative balancing act struck the "Apostle of Freedom," Thomas Jefferson, "like an alarm bell in the night," filling him with terror – in his telling – knowing that the stakes and level of conflict over slavery would only to rise.

The Wilmot Proviso in Congress following the Mexican War, a generation later, was a measure introduced and reintroduced to simply exclude slavery from any new territory accruing from that conflict. Though it never passed, such a proposal was anathema and terrifying to the South; its very existence solidified that section's hard and fast defensive resolve.

By the Kansas-Nebraska Act of 1854, the southerners and those standing with them for fear of provoking them to secession managed to adjust the Missouri Compromise line northward to the boundary between the so-named territories, pending a referendum in the case of Kansas, the more settled of the two. That measure set off a deadly blood feud to pack the raw frontier territory with slavery proponents and its bitter opponents. The founding of fortified rival territorial governments and sporadic guerilla warfare produced the all-out killing zone that came to be known as "bleeding Kansas."

Out of that intense, surreal experience surged the half-crazed militant abolitionist John Brown, with his plot to raid the government arsenal at Harpers Ferry, Virginia (now West Virginia). Brown planned to arm and inspire all the slaves in the South to stand up and take their freedom.

He was captured and hanged, but became a holy martyr, paying the ultimate price for all those too apathetic, or too lily-livered.

The stage was set for determined action by Harriet Beecher Stowe's melodramatic Uncle Tom's Cabin (1851). Stowe had drawn a bright moral line for conscionable Americans, something it may have taken another member of American humanity to do.

Ultimately, there was the real life moral outrage to come to grips with of the Taney Supreme Court's decision in *Dred Scott v. Sanford* (1857).[65]

---

[64] See Ralph Emerson Twitchell, *The Military Occupation of the Territory of New Mexico, from 1846 to 1851*, (Santa Fe: Sunstone Press, 2007).

This so-called Dred Scott Decision held that the government had no power whatsoever to ban slavery in any territory. Thus, the practice most repugnant to America's founding *creed* was legalized throughout the American territorial empire. The decision further held that escaped slaves were to be seized and returned from *anywhere.* *

---

[65] Otherwise noteworthy: Judge Shaw of the Massachusetts bench ruled that "the labor union in and of itself" was "not illegal". See *Commonwealth v. Hunt*, 4 Metcalf III (Mass., 1842). Not magnanimous. But, at least, a step.

Part 6 – Breaking and Taping the China – 1860 to 1898

In order to achieve anything by normal political means, a leader has to have sufficient support, or at least acquiescence, from *whoever* controls sovereign power in the country governed by the particular decision. The argument of some that President Lincoln was responsible for an unnecessarily catastrophic Civil War – because he could have abolished slavery, the splinter causing the festering of North-South relations, by means other than a war – is mistaken on a number of counts.

Thomas DiLorenzo advances such an argument in his book The Real Lincoln and in other writings; "the Copperhead" (Confederate-sympathizing northern) writer Henry Clay Dean, in the immediate post-Civil War era, also faulted and defamed Lincoln for alleged arbitrariness in forcibly overthrowing the sovereign will of the southern people and states.[66]

But, on the one hand, a majority of white southerners (to say *nothing* of the whole southern population) didn't want the South to secede, but were *forced* along. And on the other hand, white southerners in general after the war didn't actually feel toward Lincoln the way DiLorenzo and Dean suggest. Lincoln gained a large measure of acceptance – not to say popularity – in the South in the post-war era, when, as one historian put it, "Most southerners came to believe that Lincoln's secretary of war [Edwin M. Stanton] was a disaster to the South", and a great many came to blame the excesses in the fighting on [him].[67]

The *pre-war* South, even discounting the fact that its enfranchised white males made up only a small minority of its population, was not a particularly democratic society. In fact, the miniscule minority were major slaveholders in the decades prior to the outbreak of the Civil War. They had managed to control the somewhat larger minority who were politically enfranchised, channeling the conversation to the extent of successfully painting people in favor of the emancipation of slaves in the southern mind as dangerous radicals, more *sub-human* than the lowly, despised blacks they sought to free.

Abolitionists were tagged with threatening the liberty of *self-rule* in the region, as well as unleashing the specter of *terrorism* in the form of liberated *fiends* roaming the land raping and pillaging. Anti-slavery thus came to be

---

[66] Thomas J. DiLorenzo, *The Real Lincoln*, (New York: Three Rivers Press, 2002), p. 33.

[67]; Henry Clay Dean, *Crimes of the Civil War*, (Baltimore: Inesz Co., 1868), pp. 25 ff., 412 ff.; Michael Davis, *The Image of Lincoln in the South*, (Knoxville: Univ. of Tennessee Press, 1971), pp. 136-7.

viewed as *beyond the pale*, and blacks not even *subject to consideration* in the proposition, *"all men are created equal,"* but as posing serious threats to the happy southern way of life. Such ruminations came to dominate southern political discourse.

Second, the contention that Lincoln and the North could have abolished slavery piecemeal – because opportunities had arisen to liberate small groups of slaves in a particular locality or by category in one or another marginal state, and this could eventually have resulted in freeing all or practically all slaves short of abolishing the institution itself (which was something the controlling minority in the South was *determined never to permit*) – is absurd.

Third, emancipating the slave population – though it became one of Lincoln's objectives late in the war – was not initially among his motivations and was only adopted as an objective when it had become politically feasible.

Quakers were the anti-slavery *pioneers* in the South as in the North, followed by many of the Methodist clergy. But, in the latter case, influential laymen started showing up at conferences of the clergy demanding repeal of anti-slavery proclamations and rulings, lest all financial support and state favor would cease, with stronger measures hinted at.

In the South, the abolitionists became outcasts and found that their numbers did not grow. In the North, meanwhile, surprisingly similar tactics worked, but only for a limited time.[68]

The results were predictable: a particularly astute observer, in retrospect, wrote that "the white people of the South are essentially a fine, kindly breed... perhaps their early and fatal mistake was that they refused long before the Civil War to allow the South differences of opinion... Men act as they do in the South, they murder, they lynch, they insult, because they listen to but one side of a question."[69]

And while the economics of slavery and slave loss were an effective consideration only for the limited number who owned slaves, or otherwise profited from their labor, one motive to closed-mindedness on the subject was the frequently reinforced fear of a general slave insurrection, leading to pressure in Congress and sentiment in society for strong fugitive slave laws. Related fears of black male sexual prowess and intent were also involved. Poor-soil or naturally isolated counties and localities in the South, such as

---

[68] H. Sheldon Smith, *In His Image, But..., Racism in Southern Religion, 1789-1910*, (Durham, NC: Duke Univ. Press, 1972), p. 23 ff.
[69] W.E.B. DuBois, *Black Reconstruction*, quoted in David Grimsted, *American Mobbing, 1828-1861*, (New York: Oxford Univ. Press, 1998), p. 114; Clement Eaton, *The Freedom of Thought Struggle in the Old South*, (New York: Harper-Collins, 2000), p. 114 ff.

eastern Tennessee or Jones County, Mississippi, with few slaves, where these arguments didn't apply, stood apart during the war as areas of Unionist sentiment.

But, anti-slavery was a sensitive subject in the North as well. Early on, in the early 1830s, a serial debate, over several evenings, on the subject of abolition by Lane Seminary students and other associated – among whom were celebrated abolitionists later – in Cincinnati, a northern city, led to actual riots.[70]

It has been the fashion, to defame him, to claim that Lincoln was not interested in emancipation, at least for its own sake.[71] But, this is contrary to what the southern secession commissioners in the various states thought, and what became the primary motivation for their action of leaving the union and rejoining defensively to form the Confederacy. They reacted thus and powerfully against the threat they saw in Lincoln as anointed head of the triumphant Republican Party, with its "frightening" slogan: "Free Soil, Free Labor, Free Men."

Indeed, Lincoln was *not* active as an abolitionist pre-war, as is often pointed out. But, there is much anecdotal and some documentary evidence to support his claim that he was indeed, in his words, "naturally, anti-slavery," a man bearing a sentiment awaiting circumstances favorable to its expression.[72]

So, did Lincoln choose the war? Yes, but only in preference to dissolving the union. Was he given a chance to negotiate or navigate to an alternative? Unfortunately not. Southern apologists and revisionists claim that the war was fought to protect southern self-rule, hence for liberty and democracy, both strong American values! (In so claiming, they *ignore* that the Founders deliberately began the Constitution with the words, *"We the people,"* not *"We the states assembled."*

And they ignore that the only southern choice questioned was that of treating human beings as property and holding them as livestock. Could not a state have just as rationally passed legal rules regarding permissible murder (taking of life) as permissible slavery (taking of liberty and preventing the pursuit of happiness)? For *whose benefit* was slavery to be sanctioned? Not for the national benefit or due to democratic demand, but, finally, only for a *selfish few*, who saw fit to plunge the nation into a bloody catastrophe and wreck the constitution of the Founding Fathers they claimed to revere, and copied in their own separate constitution. In reality, just to benefit *themselves*

---

[70] See David Grimsted, op. cit., pp. 42-43, 61.

[71] See Thomas DiLorenzo, *The Real Lincoln*, pp. 10 ff., 54 ff.; Charles E. Dew, *Apostles of Disunion*, (Charlottesville: Univ. Press of Virginia, 2001), pp. 44, 74 ff; Eric Foner, *Free Soil, Free Labor, Free Men*, (New York: Oxford Univ. Press, 1995).

[72] See Peter Burchard, *Lincoln and Slavery*, (New York: Athenium, 1999), pp. 1-11.

at whatever cost exacted from everyone else, their patron saint being *St. Samson.*

Another question entirely was whether those same oligarchic southern states, constrained to ignore the righteousness of slavery by emphasizing the very *worst-case* scenario of the consequences of ending it, possessed the constitutional right to dissolve the union. One view among historians is that the reason Jefferson Davis, the Confederate president, escaped trial for treason once captured (disguised as a woman) was that "the federal government knew that it could not try Davis for treason without raising the *constitutional issue of secession.*"[73]

A thorny question though that may or may not be, it obviously could not be accomplished without deliberately inflicting damage on the prevailing union and legitimate constitutional system.

Lincoln, as is well known, did not win a *majority* of the popular vote nationwide in the 1860 election, but only in the North. The Democrats had finally split irreconcilably, North and South, and so fielded two candidates, dashing whatever chance they had of holding onto power. Further complicating matters, a conciliatory party arose – *Constitutional Union* – fielding a *fourth* candidate.

The ideology and platform of the Republicans, who nominated Lincoln, avowedly did not favor abolition, only limiting slavery to states and territories where it already existed.[74]

Yet the southern secessionists were undeniably correct that the position of the Republican Party, amounting to *curtailing* the extension of slavery, would doom that institution and the lifestyle dependent on it. Because, new states assuredly would be added, and their elected representatives would, if free by law, help extinguish slavery.

Lincoln, of course, never would have been nominated had he been an ardent and active abolitionist. In 1860, the North would not have embraced a candidate espousing abolition, partly because such an uncompromising position would guarantee dissolution of the union. But, in addition,

---

[73] Edward K. Eckert, in *Charles Adams, When in the Course of Human Events, Arguing the Case of Southern Secession*, (Lanham, MD: Rowan and Little, 2000), p. 17.

[74] Eric Foner, op. cit., pp. 301-302. Foner cites I.F. Stone's observation that "The Republican Party succeeded by soft-pedaling the issue of slavery altogether and concentrating on economic issues which would attract Northern businessmen and Western farmers." See I.F. Stone, "Party of the Rich and Well-Born," (New York Review of Books, June 20, 1968), p. 34.

northerners also tended not to be favorably disposed to blacks, either, and many had serious reservations concerning their nature.

Frederick Douglass, an eloquent freed black who had become a leading abolitionist and managed, tellingly, to develop a friendship with the president that got him received at the White House, feared that Lincoln might not *ever* emancipate the slaves, and might use slavery's limited survival as a bargaining chip to end the war with the union restored.

But, instead, Douglass's and the abolitionists' hopes were at last *rewarded* once Lincoln had already in effect secured victory, and so could abolish slavery without bringing about political disaster. It seemed almost as though Douglass had finally talked him into it![75]

Meanwhile, the absence of the previous southern intransigence in Congress during the war years – an intransigence on myriad questions maintained primarily on behalf of a small elite group (the large landed estate owners who had captured exclusive control of southern thought and sovereignty) – was *gone* after the southerners removed themselves. And their unfortunate departure was exploited to good advantage by the remaining members, on behalf of the broader national interest.

Results included such initiatives as abundant homesteads in the West, land grant colleges, and a transcontinental railroad with an advantageous central route, all of which would have been very different with federal power *rejected out of hand*.[76]

But the southern *antifederalist* ideologues were not the *only* foes of true constitutional democracy and the enactment of much of the American *creed* that Lincoln encountered as president.

An interesting alleged quote, often cited by people who find political and economic domination by corporate power to be injurious to *"We, the people,"* and pronounced a fake most often by those who find that OK, is from a letter allegedly written by President Lincoln to a Col. William F. Elkins on November 21, 1864. In it, Lincoln intimates that, "I see in the near future a crisis approaching that unnerves me and causes me to tremble for the safety of my country... corporations have been enthroned and an era of corruption in high places will follow, and the money power of the country will endeavor to

---

[75] Paul Kendrick and Stephen Kendrick, *Douglass and Lincoln*, (New York: Walker & Company, 2008). For an example of the line that Lincoln reluctantly embraced emancipation as a political ploy, see DiLorenzo, *The Real Lincoln*, p. 33 ff.

[76] The Gadsden Purchase from Mexico of 1853, south of the Mexican Cession lands, for the purpose of providing a transcontinental rail route linking the South to the west coast as a condition, compared to the actual, more central, route chosen, is emblematic of antebellum southern control and intent.

prolong its reign by working upon the prejudices of the people until all wealth is aggregated in a few hands and the Republic is destroyed. I feel at this moment more anxiety for the safety of my country than ever before, even in the midst of war. God grant that my suspicion may prove groundless."[77]

All one can conclude is that, even if the letter itself is fraudulent, the conditions and happenings it portends for the then-future *are all too real.*

And there was *plenty* in Lincoln's experience with potent private self-interests in restraint of the general welfare that we can authenticate.

The British banks, during Lincoln's tenure, were actively *financing the Confederacy* (It was, reportedly, the idea of the Rothschilds – the controllers of British banking – to encourage a split in the North American colossus and very lucratively *finance both sides* of the great struggle that would ensue).

When Lincoln entered the White House, with the war starting, a combination of the large Eastern banks anonymously affiliated with the ever-interested British and international bankers, offered a loan package to finance the war effort that was "little short of extortion." $150 million – a staggering sum then – was advanced at interest rates of 24% to 36%.

Lincoln's response, partly because he was left with no alternative that wouldn't bankrupt and mortgage the country, was the creation of the *federal government-issued* United States Notes (or "Greenbacks"). These were the brainchild of Henry Carey, later sneeringly referenced as "Lincoln's 'economy guru'". These notes the government didn't have to purchase or borrow at interest from *anyone*. In fact, they seemed to be exactly what the Constitution mandated – except that they were backed by human labor rather than specie, which might have created a quibble. Initially found constitutional,

---

[77] Emannuel Hertz, *Abraham Lincoln: A New Portrait*, Vol. 2, (New York: Liveright, 1931), p. 954. Those who declare the quotation a fake declare it so partly because they say they say they cannot find any record elsewhere of a Col. William F. Elkins. But, they possibly didn't look in Lincoln's law partner, William H. Herndon's <u>Life of Lincoln</u>. My copy was published by The World Publishing Company, Cleveland, 1930. On page 138, it lists a "Wm. F. Elkin". There's no "s" in the name, to be sure, but quite possibly, an old friend of Lincoln's, and more than possibly, the same person. The deniers don't prove the letter a fraud, but only reiterate that it hasn't been established as authentic. An anecdote oft repeated is that the letter's possessor won't release it to specialists. But, that wouldn't necessarily be because the he doubts its authenticity or knows it's a fake, but only that he doesn't want to put its likely worth at risk that it might not be genuine.

they were phased out after Lincoln's passing.[78] *But they got the country through the war.*[79]

And, once again, European (especially British) financiers were thrown into a tizzy by what they derisively termed American *go-it-aloneism*. An 1865 London Times editorial reads:

"If the mischievous financial policy which had its origin in the North American Republic during the late war in that country, should become indurated down to a fixture, then that Government will furnish its own money without cost. It will pay off it[s] debts and be without debt. It will become prosperous beyond precedent in the history of the civilized world. The brains and wealth of all countries will go to North America. That government must be destroyed or it will destroy every monarchy on the globe."[80]

Out of all of President Lincoln's beautiful phrasings and eloquence – providing the *other* measure of his leadership against damning odds, in addition to his noted wisdom and firmness – a select few examples stand out as not just throw-away lines, but meriting *creedal* status.

One, with certainly, is his formula calling for the preservation of the *"government of the people, by the people, and for the people"*, which – *phenomenally* – reiterates and enhances the following tenets: *"freedom to control the government"* (popular sovereignty), *"freedom from government control"* (by stating who the government is *for* and to whom the government belongs), *"liberty and justice for all"* (as the *purpose* for a government), *"all men [people] are created equal"* (by not mentioning prevailing classes among the people), and *"personal and national independence"* (desiring that it be continued).

Another provisional tenet, set down in his Second Inaugural Address, *"With malice toward none,"* has been adopted (way too) optimistically: Taking it as *descriptive* projects us, unworthily, as it turns out, as reliably *"the good guys,"* above reasonable suspicion of ever being guilty of the really dastardly things that we know *others* are capable of. Many continue to subscribe to this notion, which actually stems (*or, would stem, if true*) from a proper recognition that "all *people*" – not just all American citizens, *really are created equal and endowed...*

And it seems as well that we've misconstrued, or completely lost from sight, Lincoln's immortal *"a just and lasting peace"* as a serious objective.

---

[78] See Otto Gresham, <u>The Greenbacks</u>, (Decatur, MI: Invictus, 1927), p. 193.
[79] Ellen Hodgson Brown, op. cit., pp. 91-93, citing Ron Kirby, "Dead Presidents' Society," Feb. 6, 2007, Germany's Chancellor Bismarck remarked in an 1876 interview: "The death of Lincoln was resolved upon" (i.e., in connection).
[80] Ibid. 2007, et al.

Instead, for hidden, sinister, and *unworthy* reasons, we seem to pick deadly fights around the globe on the slightest (even bogus) pretexts.

So, was an international conspiracy really behind the demise of Lincoln, as Bismarck's remark [see footnote above] infers? Or, was it the classic "lone gunman," the member of a local sort of al-Qaeda of dead-enders who were paradoxically fully capable in and of themselves without any state sponsorship?[81]

As it turned out, Lincoln's assassin or assassins created a martyr, but one lacking sufficient residual power to command the paramount objective of a restored happy and amicable union of all the states, working together to extend civil rights, justice, and equal citizenship to all, black and white. *"With malice toward none"* never entered the waking world in America in practical politics or policy. Instead, the blunt tools imposed for well-intended Reconstruction (federal occupation and sanctions on the South) sowed the seeds of bitterness and distrust, the harvest of which still blights the nation's landscape.

Some elements of the legacy of these policies of coercion and punishment have been exaggerated sectionalism and divided politics, skewed opposite views of history and public national institutions, Jim Crow, the Ku Klux Klan and lynching, segregation laws, mandatory court orders, and separate development, phobias, religious extremism, and an increase of emphasis on militarization of life.

Put in the simplest of terms: beginning in 1865, with the ascent of Andrew Johnson, Lincoln's unity-ticket loyal southern (from Tennessee) 1864 running-mate to the presidency, a stand-off developed. The two sides were factions within the federal government on the questions of black citizenship and rights and the status going forward of the southern states.

The so-called "Radical Republicans" in Congress – formerly the spearheads of abolitionism – demanded and voted for full equality and suffrage (voting rights) for former slaves, requiring only that they be male and of the approved voting age.

But President Johnson, a former Tennessee Senator, and his less-numerous and more-conservative cohorts, were sympathetic first and foremost to the desires of the longtime citizens of the southern states. They wanted to leave the questions of equality and suffrage up to the respective states, basically as they had been before the war, without slavery as such.

The good patrons of those states voiced their desire – reasonably enough – above all, to avoid being governed by uneducated former slaves. In order to

---

[81] Other theories point to members of the Confederate cabinet, or disabused members of Lincoln's own circle.

dramatize this rather fearsome, seemingly even irrational, imperative of the South, the District of Columbia quickly organized a non-binding referendum among its white citizens on whether its black residents ought to be permitted to register and vote. The resulting tally was a resounding 35 in favor, and 6,931 against.[82] But, was it just the *education factor*, or something else in the southern imagination at work in resisting the possibility of black participation?

The Radical Republicans, representing New England and areas and states directly to the west, largely settled by New Englanders, pushed through their "Reconstruction Act," requiring military occupation of the South to enforce civil rights and the suffrage of blacks, and Andrew Johnson vetoed it as well as other portions of the Reconstruction program, declaring that there was *no Reconstruction* (or correction of past injustices); there was only moving forward. This led, indirectly, to his impeachment for obstructionism. He was barely acquitted by the Senate, but his vetoes overridden.

And the South *did* come to be ruled and represented largely by its resident Republicans, virtually all black, aided by federal patronage appointees, who came to be called "Carpetbaggers" and were bitterly resented for preventing the literate white southern community from running its own affairs, including managing relations with and placing customary restrictions on less-qualified blacks.

A reasonable read might be that what President Lincoln intended to achieve was an *actualization of* what has come to be known as the doctrine of "*American Exceptionalism,*" with the character of American society *actually being* exceptional. This he proposed to accomplish by creating what the tenets of America's revolutionary *creed* clearly called for – an independent, politically inclusive nation practicing equality and justice. The *perfection* of that actualization, he must have known, still lay in the future, beyond many Americans' current capacity or disposition. But an *approximation* was clearly needed "*to bind up the nation's wounds.*" The difference Lincoln's personal leadership would have made nationwide in effecting this, had he lived, is impossible to know.

Many were asking in the midst of 1865 – with the war freshly won and President Lincoln dead a month or so – was the obstinate new southern president of the U.S. going to take the victory, so bloody and hard-won by the union armies, and simply *give it back* to the defeated South?[83] The intent of Congress, three-fourths Republican – the party of "free men, free labor, and free soil" – was to *reverse* the 1857 Dred Scott decision, giving as it had each

---

[82] Eric Foner, _Reconstruction, America's Unfinished Revolution, 1863-1877_, (New York: Harper & Row, 1988), pp. 239-240.

[83] See Garret Epps, _Democracy Reborn_, (New York: Henry Holt, 2006), p. 38.

state separately power to grant or deny liberty to its inhabitants. Congress's remedy was a new constitutional amendment and attendant legislation and enforcement erasing Dred Scott as a blot on the body politic.

Such was the nature of the program put forth by the Reconstruction Congress, the Fourteenth Amendment boldly guaranteeing civil rights and full citizenship to all native-born adult Americans. Period. (But notoriously *excluding* women and Indians).

And, as long as the federal government enforced the fundamental law with troops, courts, and police power across the South, civil rights for former slaves bloomed on the heels of the Civil War. Black southern governors, black members of Congress, all Republican – black freedom – blossomed in every eventually readmitted southern state, for awhile. And southern tempers seethed.

President Ulysses S. Grant kept the occupation force in place for his two terms, after Johnson's one.

And then, with the 1876 election for president in dispute, with the Democratic candidate Samuel Tilden the presumptive winner, winning in the popular count and needing only one of twenty-two disputed electoral votes in three southern states (including Florida), and set to represent his base – largely in the South – in his presidency, northern politicians crafted a deal. The three southern states threw their disputed electoral votes to Rutherford Hayes, the Republican, in exchange for giving control back to whites in the South by removing the federal troops.[84] And thus, Jim Crow – the mechanism of white power – was born and white supremacy became the ruling creed of the South, the American *creed* born of the Revolution be damned.

Meanwhile, all across the western plains, the genocide of and wholesale theft of land from Native Americans, ongoing for generations, was continuing, and rapidly picking up speed, a larger percentage of Indians perishing in these wars and outright atrocities than of Jews exterminated [in Europe] by Hitler.[85]

In November of 1864, with half a year of the Civil War still remaining and the South just about played out, Colonel John Milton Chivington of the Third Colorado Voluntary Army, a former Methodist minister and aspiring politician, was locked in the very midst of what could be called a hundred-day *hecatomb* (the *hundred days* coinciding with the period of his volunteers' enlistments). In this time, he confronted, seeking *extermination*, a peaceful Cheyenne and

---

[84] See Page Smith, *Trial by Fire, A People's History of the Civil War and Reconstruction*, (New York: McGraw-Hill, 1982), pp. 919-931.
[85] Peter Dale Scott, "Two Indonesias, Two Americas," (ConsortiumNews.com, June 9, 1998).

Arapaho village at a spot called Sand Creek. The commander's *instruction* to his troops was: "Kill and scalp all, little and big... Nits make lice."[86]

It's true that violent fringe characters may surface in any war. But this impulse to kill as good sport... the spirit of "*I love to be wading in gore*," (also quoted of this same commander), had rolled straight up the American plains from George Washington and the Cape Fear first colonists on, to and past the Rockies. "Any man who kills a hostile Indian is a patriot," had declared the Governor of Colorado. The whites of the region were called upon to "organize [themselves] to pursue, kill, and destroy."

Lean Bear, a prominent Cheyenne peace advocate, was murdered on sight. Ten of the twenty-seven stories concerning Indians in the Denver press during 1863 had favored "extermination." Early in the campaign, Chivington's regiment of volunteers came up dry and was roasted as a laughingstock: "the bloodless Third." *That* sort of treatment couldn't stand.

The biblically multitudinous bison were destroyed to starve and neuter the Indian. And later came Custer's own hecatomb. And thereupon, followed the atrocity visited at Wounded Knee.

There were also troubles tolerating Chinese workers brought in to work on western railroads and in mines. Immigration became a highly sensitive subject.

As Walt Whitman wrote: "The word democracy is a great word whose history remains unwritten. That history has yet to be enacted."[87] But even the idealistic Whitman was not convinced of the practicality of expanding democracy – a prospect apparently in view. "I will not gloss over the appalling dangers of universal suffrage in the United States," he wrote in Democratic Vistas in 1871, (presciently, three years after passage of the enabling Fourteenth Amendment).

All the while, the women's suffrage crusaders were at work, taking up the lance from the abolitionists, though relations were not always entirely warm between the two movements. In particular, the suffragettes were piqued when the Fourteenth Amendment didn't include women. But, still, the likes of Susan B. Anthony, Elizabeth Cady Stanton, Lucy Stone, and Carrie Chapman Catt were well-known figures and were making headway opinion-wise. Black activist Sojourner Truth was also on the trail for the women's vote, as were some notable men.

---

[86] Ward Churchill, *A Little Matter of Genocide*, (San Francisco: City Lights, 1997), pp. 228-233. See also Helen Hunt Jackson, *A Century of Dishonor [1880]*, (New York: Indian Head Books, 1994), p. 66 ff, 343 ff.

[87] Walt Whitman, *Complete Poetry and Selected Prose*, (New York: Library of America, 1982), p. 960.

On the political front, the first real women's suffrage breakthrough came when a tall and stout pioneer woman named Esther Hobart Morris, who had heard Susan Anthony speak in Illinois, moved in 1868 to South Pass, a gold mining town in Wyoming – another, and brand-new, territory that certainly experienced its share of Indian resistance.

Mrs. Morris invited influential legislators to her home and repeated the *suffragette* message she had heard to them, and got them to arrange passage of the same in Wyoming, a first in the nation. Utah Territory followed a few months later. And soon thereafter, sturdy Esther Morris served her community as America's first female justice of the peace.[88]

The giant businesses growing up in that day – no doubt following the example of the transcontinental railroad companies, starting on a gigantic scale in the late 1860s – became cozy with the Republican Party and the closely associated federal government. Grover Cleveland, of Buffalo, New York, the only Democrat-elected president in that era, was approved as being acceptably pro-northern. The Populist movement of the time, important as a generator of ideas, was mainly an agrarian and western miner affair, and eventually touted coinage exclusively of abundant western silver, domestically produced, which could have provided expanded real backing for currency – something which, *significantly*, the banking and establishment class roundly rejected.

As things stood, the more "extreme" Populist Party (a third-party successor to the earlier Greenback Party), surged in popularity with the publication and circulation of the meaty pamphlet Coin's Financial School. In a slightly more-lasting sense, the more-or-less *fringe* Populists temporarily served to remove the left wing stigma – an association with the bogeymen of the day – *anarchists*, and assorted not quite respectable *labor unionists* and radical farmers – from the mainline Democrats.[89]

As corporations in the major industries (steel, petroleum, industrial chemicals, building materials, food processing, communications, as well as the railroads) continued to grow in wealth and power, investigative journalists, such as Horace Greeley, Jacob Riis, E.W. Scripps, Joseph Pulitzer, William Randolph Hearst, and numerous others, known at the time as "muckrakers," explored the intriguing behavior of them and their principal owners (the "robber barons") and sought to uncover for the public their underhanded or questionable dealings.

---

[88] Miriam Gurko, op. cit., p. 228.

[89] Robert C. McMath, *American Populist, A Social History*, (New York: Hill and Wang, 1992), pp. 143 ff, 200; Ellen Hodgson Brown, op. cit., p. 113 ff; William H. Harvey, _Coin't Financial School_, (Coin Publishing Company, 1894).

The investigative papers were still in those days independent operators who used and shamelessly abused their popular oversight of the industrialists and society's "high rollers" to become wealthy and famous themselves. Owing to their independence, they performed an invaluable service to patrons and voting public in late nineteenth-century America.

In sync with "informed" public opinion, early national legislation to try to exercise some control over the new corporate interests, during a period of fluctuating majorities in Congress, included the Sherman Anti-Trust Act of 1887 and the Interstate Commerce Act of 1890, asserting federal government oversight in most instances.

A monumental *contrary* U.S. Supreme Court case, as it's customarily portrayed, decided in 1886, was that of *Santa Clara County v. Southern Pacific Railroad.*

Santa Clara was superficially a rather mundane case in terms of what it directly decided, and unexceptional in its conclusion. Yet it is frequently cited as laying down the precedent for the monumental tenet that corporations are included as *persons* under the equal protection clause of the Fourteenth Amendment. *Ipso facto*, corporations are legally *persons*, possessing all the same rights.

And therein lay a world of trouble and hurt for the United States. Because, thus endowed as *citizens*, corporations – as they've grown enormously in financial heft – have increasingly drawn all the oxygen out of the economy. Not properly restrained as society's *tools*, rather than the members constituting it, they have irresistibly subverted our politics and law, assumed control of our natural environment, and conditioned our every personal act, further blunting and countering the operation of the our *creed*, i.e., the ubiquitous "what sets us apart" (supposedly and intentionally) as a nation of individuals.[90]

Ohioan *William McKinley* was the last Civil War veteran to serve as president. His election (1896) was considered pivotal, bringing the Republicans back to *solid power* for the first time in two decades. His administration marked the debut of the United States as a major diplomatic and military power. *And what a debut it was.*[91]

---

[90] *Santa Clara County v. Southern Pacific Railroad*, 118 U.S. 394 (1886).
[91] See Kevin Philips, *William McKinley*, ((New York: Times Books, 2003), Introduction.

Part 7 – Shattering the Idols – 1898 to 1919

The entrance to the Twentieth Century began in 1898 in a big way. 1898, the second year of William McKinley's securely Republican presidency, was the year that the American republic started to come into its own (according to some), having overcome the *ridiculous,* potentially limiting Populist-Democratic notion of depending on abundant silver specie, perhaps *along with* far-scarcer gold, to provide a substantial basis for spendable wealth. Instead, McKinley's election over William Jennings Bryan was construed as a re-endorsement of mysteriously bank-created lightly backed money and credit at interest, permitting the country to flex its economic muscles more feely.

Now more than three decades out from a good, clarifying wartime scourging, the interests charged with the control of public information – captured as their messenger service of late by the financial establishment – started (once admitted to power) ramping up for *war*. The understanding is, if there is not already a dispute that qualifies as a pretext in the offing, they will conjure one up! Because *war* opens the heavens to replenish to *overflowing* commercial and financial coffers and solidifies their power and connections.

Accordingly, a long anticipated buildup was percolating in late 1890s America, a country stirring again, which hadn't counted coup, or added an inch to its extent, except questionably with Alaska, in two generations. But now, there were causes afoot. And it was time to unleash the nation's growing strength.

1898 was an exciting year, a year full of surprises. A half decade earlier, American sugar planters had begun to take over the fabric of Hawaii, Pacific islands regarded as grown-up America's proper staging area for trade and interaction with the storied East, the goal of the enterprise that had spawned America, it was recalled, since before the days of Columbus.

In July of 1898, a core of thirty patriotic American planters forced the abdication of the sitting Hawaiian monarch, founded their own short-lived Republic of Hawaii, and proudly handed over sovereignty to the United States. The right of the Hawaiians to run and possess their own lives in their own smaller, ancient country in their own preferred way was simply too inconvenient to take seriously.[92]

Sugar had never tasted so sweet! In the early winter months at the start of the same year, Americans began learning preparatorily of the rueful fate of Cubans who were rising up to free themselves from the last vestiges of once-great Spanish colonial power in the hemisphere. Intrepid reporter William Randolph Hearst went to Cuba to see and flamboyantly report the oppression

---

[92] See Stephen Kinzer, <u>Overthrow</u>, (New York: Times Books, 2006), pp. 9-30.

and attendant misery of its hapless victims day after day in his <u>New York Journal</u> and string of wholly-owned affiliates.[93]

One of President McKinley's strongest conservative Republican allies, Senator Redfield Proctor of Vermont, also journeyed to Cuba and reported his observations to his colleagues and the readers of newspaper articles throughout the country.

Not a man normally to be carried away by compassion, Senator Proctor described conditions in the rising Cuban countryside as follows: "It is not peace, nor is it war. It is desolation, misery, and starvation."

The "re-concentration camps" for punishing rebels were "virtually prison yards," Senator Proctor cried out, with women and children forced at gunpoint to live in filth and despair. "Torn from their homes," "with foul earth, foul air, foul water, and foul food or none, what wonder that one-half have died and one-quarter of the living are so diseased that they cannot be saved? ... Little Children are still walking around with arms and chest terribly emaciated, eyes swollen and abdomen bloated to three times the natural size... [etc.]"

Americans were aghast, and increasingly unsure what steps to take to stay true to their "values."[94]

McKinley, who famously despised war, dispatched – after a great deal of inside discussion and planning, and then too much fanfare – the battleship *Maine* to Havana harbor to overawe the incorrigible Spanish authorities and induce them to change their ways, or just get out. It was something of a throwback to Commodore Perry's gunboat diplomacy that succeeded in opening up stubborn Japan to outside trade in 1853.

Suddenly, on February 15 of that fateful year, the mighty *Maine* exploded and sunk in the harbor. And the response was to blame the Spanish for it, even without proof.

In fact, it was equally possible that the explosion was an accident, caused by an undetected fire in the ship's coal department, or even that the Americans blew up the *Maine* as a pretext, in order to blame the Spanish for it and provoke the American public to demand action.

And demand they did. In response, the president requested that Congress appropriate $50 million straight from the U.S. Treasury – *without borrowing anything* – to finance military action. It was, in a stroke of genius, called the "Fifty-Million-Dollar Bill," and reportedly, the Spanish were *impressed*, but

---

[93] Ibid., p. 36.
[94] David Traxel, <u>1898</u>, (New York: Knopf, 1998), pp. 116-117.

didn't pack up and stand clear. There was much excitement in the coming days about them recruiting European allies and starting a much-larger war.[95]

The morning that word of the *Maine*'s explosion and sinking reached the White House, by cable from Havana ahead of the censors, the news set off a flurry of activity. Commodore Dewey was cabled, ordering him to gather together the *Asiatic Squadron* in Hong Kong to prepare for an offensive against the Spanish in the Philippines in the likely event of a declaration.

Other squadron commanders around the world were wired requesting them to fill their holds with coal, and wires were sent to naval buyers stationed globally to obtain all of the fuel they could. Rendezvous points for scattered vessels and contingents were named. Ammunition in unprecedented quantities was placed on order. Guns needed to convert yachts and commercial vessels to warships were ordered and inventoried. And requests were sent to both houses of Congress for bills authorizing recruitment. In short, Spain's name was mud.[96]

Cuban resistance to Spanish rule was endemic, and American interest in the island – including possibly adding it to the southern slave empire – went back decades, and there had had been a number of prior war scares involving Spain.

Once war was joined in Cuba by U.S. invasion in late April, the war lasted a total of ten weeks, including San Juan Hill and all, and the U.S. forces won all the battles.

In addition, Puerto Rico was occupied practically without resistance, and Spain's occupation of the Philippines, dating back to the sixteenth century, was brought to an end by a landing and "summary" (only a little) violence. And American administration of all of these new far-flung possessions was begun, presumably not to last.[97]

An interesting sidelight of the Spanish-American War involves a rather comical example of what is called a *"false flag"* operation, a deceitful and potentially inhuman and even treasonous tactic obviously already back then in the playbook of U.S. government programs. On the way to Manila, spearheading the replacement of the Spanish regime in the Philippines, Brigadier General T.M. Anderson was dispatched first to the island of Guam

---

[95] Ibid., p. 116.

[96] Ibid., pp. 110-111. and Cuba.

[97] To secure Congressional support at the outset of hostilities, the McKinley administration embraced an amendment to the funding bill proposed by Senator Henry Teller of Colorado (the Teller Amendment), which foreswore any U.S. interest in annexing Cuba; though, notably, this stipulation did not apply to Puerto Rico, the Philippines, or to Guam. See Stephen Kinzer, op. cit., pp. 38-41.

in the western Pacific to vanquish the Spanish authorities and battery there, such as it was. Anderson and his contingent were being transported aboard the cruiser *Charleston*.

Finding no military presence at Agana, the capital, the contingent moved on to Fort Santa Cruz, on the other side of the small island, *flying a Japanese flag to deceive the natives and any Spanish personnel*. They found no Spanish vessels at anchor there, either, only a lone brigantine *also flying a Japanese flag!* The cruiser's commander, Captain Henry Glass, duly fired a few rounds from his three-pounders at the fort. But there was no return fire, and not a soul emerged.

Only after an irritating delay did a small boat come out. Three uniformed officers from the boat climbed up the ladder onto the *Charleston*'s deck, their leader declaring: "You will pardon our not immediately replying to your salute, but we are not accustomed to receiving salutes here and are not supplied with the proper guns for returning them."

"What salutes?" asked Glass, dumfounded.

"The salutes you fired," answered the Spanish officer.

It was later revealed that Guam had not had word from Manila since mid-April. It was eighteen months since the island had been visited by any Spanish war ship, and so did not know about the war, which was nearly over.

The next day, the convoy moved on to Manila, now flying the Stars and Stripes, the Spanish officers cheerfully riding aboard as prisoners of war. No American was left on Guam to hold or secure it, although the detention of Guam did result.[98]

The war with Spain in the Philippines involved a tussle, due to the Spanish desiring to avoid or escape a heavy indemnity. But the real struggle, which went on for years, was between the despised American occupying forces and the same Filipino rebels who had battled against the Spanish.

An unsigned letter to the editor written by "A mother in Lexington, Ky," dated February 25, 1899, posed a very good question: "In what does our treatment of the Filipinos differ from Spain's treatment of Cuba?" In other words, imperialism is imperialism, and does not add up to freedom *or express anything but the diametric opposite of any tenet of America's creed.*[99]

Regarding Cuba, busy-body "internationalists", who were angry that Cubans were so insolent as to not show gratitude to the U.S. for freeing them,

---

[98] Allan Keller, *The Spanish-American War*, (New York: Hawthorn, 1969), pp. 221-222.
[99] Murray Polner and Thomas E. Woods, Jr., *We Who Dared to Say No to War*, (New York: Basic Books, 2008), p. 97.

and stymied by the Teller Amendment, preventing American annexation, found a way to have their way anyway – the so-called "Platt Amendment" of 1900. In accordance with the Platt Amendment, put forward by Senator Thomas Platt of Connecticut, the U.S. would end its occupation once the Cubans agreed to issue a constitution that gave the U.S. veto power over Cuba's foreign relations, permitted the U.S. to control Cuba's treasury, conceded to the U.S. the right to intervene at any time to "protect" individual property and safety, and conceded the right of the U.S. to maintain military bases there. The *New York Evening Post* ran an editorial asking how U.S. government officials could continue to go to church in clear conscience after so openly lying about granting Cuba real independence.

Those same stipulations were long applied as well to govern U.S. relations with other nations throughout the Caribbean and Central America, and were the basis for a welter of *un-creed*-like interventions over many years. When President William McKinley signed the Platt Amendment into law on March 2, 1901, Cuba underwent a shudder, evoking a "storm of excitement," according to one historian.[100]

TR (Theodore Roosevelt), McKinley's vice president after his 1900 re-election, and who succeeded to the presidency following McKinley's 1901 assassination, was the hero of the famous cavalry charge up San Juan Hill in southeastern Cuba. As such, and as a convert to macho, rugged living, he was totally "bully" on the value of going to war for bringing out the best in man and country.

That sort of hawkishness, however, would end abruptly a few years later when he received word that his beloved son Quentin had been killed following the warrior life. Which is why the well-born in general are exempted from hazardous exposure in war. Because, if they themselves were the designated battle leaders, for the glory and great fun of organized killing, and were really exposed to the savagery of being suddenly ripped apart, shattered to shreds by bombs and shelling, and gutted, the adverse consequences for the warmongers would be dire. Because, their influence, if they were affected themselves by it – and for what, corporate objectives? (More on this later.) – could put a virtual end to the war financiers' very foremost venue of obscene profit and plunder and thus, their stranglehold over society and world events.

America in Roosevelt's time was shocked by the conspicuous and rapid surge to overriding power and prominence of the great industrialists, the Morgans, Carnegies, Rockefellers, and Du Ponts who were the controlling icons of the brave new corporate-leaning America.

---

[100] David F. Healy, *Drive to Hegemony, The United States in Cuba, 1898-1902,* (Madison: Univ. of Wisconsin Press, 1963).

Never one for subtleties, the populist TR's answer was to smash their monopolies – "trusts" – into slightly less unsightly, theoretically competing bits. But, certainly, the trend away from the earlier, more egalitarian economic system, with business or farm ownership and personal independence very widely available, to a system in which nearly everyone was dependent and subordinate – though avoided as a public topic in the "land of opportunity" – was obvious to all.

And so it was that access to consumer goods became the standard of success and subservience the price in this magnificent land. Feudalism, though only of a sort, was returning, swapping out the rewards of individual creativity and initiative for the vicarious worship of entertaining, but manifestly unworthy giants, vulgar heroes, anti-heroes, and icons.

The Sherman Antitrust Act, which for the first time sought to outlaw business monopolies and cartels, had actually been passed back in Congress in 1890, but was (*surpise!*) not vigorously enforced or litigated earlier. Not until Roosevelt and his successor, William Howard Taft, reversed *de facto* nullification by the plutocratic Supreme Court in refusing to enforce the law's provisions, and made it a priority. TR is also to be touted for his achievements in conservation and protection of the environment, a national priority in any age.

*   *   *

That the Ku-Klux-Klan credibly claimed five million members nationwide, with chapters in every single state and Alaska Territory in the late 1890s and early 1900s, is important. And the fact that there were very numerous incidents of selective or targeted indignity visited by members of the general population on blacks in every region of the country is by no means unimportant information.

But these facts remain incidental when one considers the much larger size of the general population. On the other hand, that community-sanctioned institutional racism was practiced to a certain extent far and wide (for example, barring "Negroes" by ordinance from remaining inside the limits of numerous small cities in the North after sundown, as well as a whole plethora of segregation laws throughout the South), bespeaks the prevalence of *attitudes* contrary to those enshrined in America's much-proclaimed and much-fought for *creed*.

The legal backstop for that ubiquitous official sanction was the U.S. Supreme Court ruling in the case of *Plessy v. Ferguson* (1892). This represented an almost certain misapplication of the Fourteenth Amendment to suit public attitudes. The case of Plessy irrationally construed the clause of the amendment to protect the claimed right of owners of businesses (*corporations*) to deal with clienteles separately, or prejudicially. That the equal protection provision of the law should apply to those otherwise apt to suffer discrimination (the very purpose of the amendment) was willfully *ignored* in that perverse, revealing 7-1 decision.[101]

In other words, the U.S. Supreme Court was not prepared to mandate the provisions of an amendment to Constitution that was contrary to what a majority of its members would have liked. But it *was* ready to maintain, with a straight face (presumably) that the amendment actually stated the virtual *opposite!* What a tangled web we weave... Jefferson, for all his alleged contradictions, would have *gasped.*

But American life, thus misconstrued, continued. In practice, America was, by the first decades of the twentieth century, well over a century behind its own cherished and sworn principles, the distance holding steady – and far from the country it fancied it was.

Though more individual states had granted women the vote by that time, the country as a whole continued to deny that morsel of equality to half or more of the adult population on the basis of gender.

The financial panic of 1907 created an increased drumbeat of pressure to force management of monetary policy and finances back into the hands of a central bank. Political problems facing the renewal of this tried and twice-extinguished rather European plan of finances were that the public disdained and feared trusts, Democratic politicians still tended to favor silver-based, or, less preferred, bimetallic currency.

And with private control over the currency overwhelmingly disfavored, a name and organizational scheme had to be arrived at that would satisfy and relieve the bill's most intransigent opponents, i.e., the public. Meaning that the preferred moniker, "central bank", was out.

Instead, a *deceptive name* was struck upon – "Federal Reserve System." It was not called a bank, because Americans tended not to trust powerful banks or their directors. The plan called for in the "reluctant" Democratic President Woodrow Wilson's "compromise" bill was to feature, in reality, a privately-owned institution, *not* part of the federal government, although made to sound as if it were.

It, in fact, did *not* feature *reserves* of gold or silver to be kept on deposit as a backup, though the name was designed to suggest that it might. Its functions were to be centralized, though with twelve regional branch banks, in order to assuage fears of concentrated power.

The *board of directors* of the cutely nicknamed *"Fed"* were to be presidential appointments (nominated by *whom?*), and reputedly, stock in

---

[101] 163 US 537 (1896); Peter Irons, op. cit., p. 222;

each of the member banks was open to foreign or foreign-subsidiary ownership (although the Fed's actual ownership has *never been revealed*).

The management of the Federal Reserve System that has evolved from the original – signed, after more than a hundred changes made in the creating legislation, by *reluctant*, newly-elected President Wilson early in 1913 – *denies* foreign ownership. All profits from the operation are to accrue to the U.S. Treasury; and yet, the government's annual purchases of money as needed from the Fed now require massive and increasing amounts to be borrowed, both domestically and from foreign sources, to pay the assessed interest, *steadily accumulating as the nation's debt*.

Thus is the very *independence* of the United States, a leading element of its all but universally acclaimed *creed*, seriously compromised.

President Wilson later, when the effect of the operations of the so-called "Federal Reserve System" on the American economy became more clear, lamented that he had hurt his country badly by accepting and promoting, *even in modified fashion*, the scheme forwarded by the country's leading bankers.[102]

America's drift toward involvement in World War I was gradual, and passions in the end conquered all else in bringing it about. It's questionable whether there needed to be a war at all from the standpoint of overt causes. The German sinking of the British passenger liner *Lusitania* in May, 1915, with more than ten percent of its passengers American, was considered one provocation. But less so when it was discovered the ship had been known by the Germans to be secretly transporting armaments.

But, from the standpoint of high finances, a war was needed to pull Americans together, lessen resistance to their programs, and provide ample opportunities for them to realize huge profits. Even before hostilities commenced in Europe, the propagandists did a *stellar* job of portraying Germany, the ancestral home of a plurality of Americans and then long considered a particularly peaceful abode of music and idealism, *as warlike and cruel*.[103]

---

[102] The act's original requirements mandating that at least some bullion must be held in reserve by member banks were eventually dropped; though the Constitution's requirement that the government itself emit the country's money was, again, ignored from the beginning. See Ellen Hodgson Brown, op. cit., pp. 126-128; Eustace Mullins, *A Study of the Federal Reserve*, (Eastford, CT: Martino, 2009). My question, once again, is, what on earth could persuade so many legislators to act so negligently?

[103] See Michael F. Connors, *Dealing in Hate, The Development of Anti-German Propaganda*, (Torrence, CA: Institute for Historical Review, 1983); H.W. Brands, Woodrow Wilson, (New York: Henry Holt, 2003), pp. 51-63, 69.

The "Fourteen Points" declaration, intended by President Wilson to guide the post-World War I peace process and shape the subsequent international world, appears well-meaning and, if followed, might have resulted in a peaceful world, making "the war to end all wars" successfully so. But, alas, the "Fourteen Points" lacked teeth.

And the final point of the fourteen, the idea of a "League of Nations", intended to extend the ideal of democracy to govern international relations, was effectively blocked from coming to full fruition by Wilson's own Congress' rejecting of U.S. membership. This was precisely because the plan the president set forth lacked what was considered an adequate mechanism for America to be able to *veto* the other nations' designs.

In other words, the interests controlling Congress considered a truly democratic international system *unacceptable*, a sort of official, effective *rejection* of the hallowed tenet that, in truth, *all men are created equal*, and to be seen as endowed with life, liberty, and the pursuit of happiness – and accordingly conceded *meaningful recognition*.[104]

---

[104] H.W. Brands, op. cit., pp. 89, 136-137.

Part 8 – Clashing with Demons – 1920 to 1945

While the Civil War had united Unionists of every stripe, nationality, and religion against the Confederacy, World War I tended to divide, to fragment.[105] The native-born tended to associate eastern and southern European immigrants, related to the recent enemy nations, with radical labor unionists and with dissident politics. These *designated bogey men,* or *scapegoats* were first identified as Anarchists and then, after 1917, with the international Communist/workers' movement.

Race riots became endemic as well, and resentful whites were the rioters, in at least twenty-nine major instances between 1898 and 1922. Most, but not all, of the instances were in the South. The first, in 1898, was an insurrection in Wilmington, North Carolina against a prominent black majority. The Tulsa race riots of 1922 climaxed the callous run, with many brutal and heartrending stops in between.

The Republicans and "normalcy" were swept back into power in the elections of 1920, with Warren G. Harding heading the ticket. Bolshevism (Soviet Communism), which had just taken power, was seen and feared as the new enemy, the high financiers and their propagandists and backers violently attacking a new economic system that seemingly had no place for their wealth concentration schemes.

During the years after the Bolsheviks seized power in Russia, as the Great War ground to an end, another, abortive war seldom mentioned in the conventional history books, that of the principal Allied powers invading northern Russia and other parts of that "evil" realm with an expeditionary force to aid the White Russian rivals of the Bolsheviks. The thin, outmanned Western forces were plagued by insubordination and an early pull out by the British, whose participation was deeply unpopular at home. Thus affected, the forces of the Allies were quickly routed by the Red Army.

But the "Red Scare" whipped up mainly to garner support for this campaign, continued to alarm Americans concerning the Soviets' malicious intent, alleged depravity, and superior acumen at subversion.

To be sure, any military advances or threats against America, when they occurred, would have had to been met and effectively countered. But the irony for many years in dealings with the Soviets was that, though our business and political leaders claimed to be confident concerning the

---

[105] See David H. Bennett, *The Party of Fear*, (Chapel Hill: Univ. of North Carolina Press, 1988), p. 183.

unmatched superiority of our economic system and social model, they were too afraid to put it to the competitive test. Instead, they had to resort to subversion and underhandedness, making straight-up competition, or even mutual adoption of better or more practical features from others' experiences, virtually impossible.

Hence, internationally, too, all men were not considered or treated as equal. Consequently, underhanded tricks and bad faith ruined our relations and influence with the Eastern Bloc countries, placing in question our moral and systemic superiority and scuttling advancement by example. The sort of practical competition of ideas we prided ourselves in was, in fact, itself generally taboo here in America when there was a real difference between ideas, and was replaced in international parlance by insults, mean tricks, and empty boasts.

If Communism wouldn't work, as many suspected, why not allow it to just run its course and prove as much, instead of being sabotaged and prevented from proving unaided its weakness as a system?

Could it have been because Western mega-companies were all too eager to take over the territory, and so involved the power of the state they heavily influenced in their bid, at immense taxpayer expense, even in non-military situations?

The limited cultural exchanges and technology transfers that simultaneously took place on a limited scale, were certainly far more appropriate (and less tension-raising and expensive) responses to the organizational differences than unremitting and endless hostility, intolerance, and saber rattling.

By May of 1920, following President Wilson's signature of the Twentieth Amendment passed by Congress in one of his administration's closing acts, topped by ratification by the requisite number of states, the right of women to vote was finally guaranteed across the country. It had only taken some eight decades (four generations) of rousing agitation, mind-bending reasoning, and campaigning to achieve the ultimate victory for all of humanity – a grudging blow if there ever was one for the American national creed's declaration of equality. *Thank you very much, America the magnanimous!*[106]

---

[106] As late at Nov. 15, 1917, 33 women were arrested for "obstructing a sidewalk" while picketing the White House to get President Wilson to support the women's vote. Sent to a workhouse in Virginia, they were badly worked over during the night, with the warden's blessing, by 40 club-wielding guards, and detained for weeks. Michael Streicher, "Woodrow Wilson and the 19th Amendment," AmericanHistory@Suite101.

By the early decades of the twentieth century, Native Americans were barely hanging on and clinging to the ropes, largely confined to desolate, godforsaken, and remote reservations, invariably among the least-desirable tracts of land in America, squalidly-treated to stinting, or stinking handouts.

Native spiritual practices were forbidden and Indian children taken away to harsh distant boarding schools, to learn Anglo-Saxon ways and values, especially disdain *for them,* and barred from speaking their languages. They were prepared for an alien, slave-like bare existence in their own country.

By 1924, Indians were declared U.S. citizens, but assigned the social status indicated above, virtually denied an identity within their own ancient nations. Such were the conditions of assimilation, the planned culmination of the systematic process commenced (ironically) by President Jefferson, twelve decades before. Formally since 1887, the distinctive status of "Indian" was not intended to long survive[107].

But then, late in the 1920s, vast amounts of uranium, coal, and petroleum were discovered on the once-thought-wastelands assigned as America's Indian holding grounds, and the decision was provisionally made to reclaim the affected lands from Indian possession, evicting the Indians, in order to add the now valuable tracts to the public domain – shades of Georgia gold.

It was subsequently found, though, that the federal treasury and highly interested private companies could realize their best returns of profitability by leaving the reservations intact. The idea then became to maintain them as sort of internal colonial Bantustans such as were organized by the white regimes as black "homelands" in parts of Africa.

Then, the terms of development and any economic arrangements desired could be imposed by the dominant culture. And, so it was that the interpreted meaning of the creedal tenet *"all men are created equal"* was yet again exposed to be, "not *other* men created equal – not even all *citizens,* just *us*."[108]

Black Americans, still living most everywhere, including across the South, under Jim Crow laws approved by the U.S. Supreme Court, were having a hard time. Woodrow Wilson openly courted black votes, where such were allowed, by pledging the first responsive ear in the White House since Cleveland.

But, in fact, once elected, he filled his administration with southerners who were deaf to black hopes and concerns. Washington, DC, offered better

---

[107] See Wilcomb E. Washburn, *The Assault on Indian Tribalism,* (Philadelphia: Lippincott, 1975).
[108] Ward Churchill, op. cit., pp. 246-247.

housing and neighborhoods for blacks than elsewhere, but also remained strictly segregated.

President Theodore Roosevelt had casually invited his last business appointment of the day, the famous black man, Booker T. Washington, to stay for dinner one day. And the *Memphis Scimitar* blasted him for it in the meanest terms, calling TR's gesture "the most damnable outrage ever."

South Carolina Senator Benjamin "Pitchfork" Tillman predicted (or *proposed?*) that the president's "entertaining that nigger will necessitate our killing a thousand niggers in the South before they will learn their place again." Such language scarcely raised an eyebrow in the country, because such outrages – *and attendant actions* – against human dignity were daily occurrences in much of the country throughout much of the first half of the twentieth century, and had been thus *for centuries* before.

Plus, nobody, it seems, thought logically or literally about the real meaning of the *creed* virtually everyone – *no doubt including "Pitchfork" Tillman* – exalted regularly in glowing terms as setting America apart from every other land on the face of the earth.[109]

As a miserably-oppressed part of the population of a supposedly free country loudly espousing equality and justice and decrying perceived injustice *wherever else* in the world, truly courageous individuals among the black population did what they could to defend their cohorts themselves.

Thus did Ida B. Wells-Barrett, a black southern schoolteacher, speak out loudly and often, beginning in the late nineteenth century and continuing for decades. In doing so, she attempted (*futilely?*) to draw the apparently sleeping nation's attention and conscience to the brutal reality of condoned public spectacle lynchings, mostly, but not solely, in the South.

Its establishment prompted by a race riot *in Lincoln's home town*, Springfield, Illinois, in 1908, the NAACP – National Association for the Advancement of Colored People – was founded on February 12, 1909. But the nationwide organization existed for several decades before even one prominent white leader had the guts, or summoned the virtue, to join. This remained the unfortunate reality for many years.

Meanwhile "Christian" white men, especially throughout the South, joined together in droves to honestly practice their "birthright" of vicious intolerance and deadly, determined opposition to their fellow citizens, who happened to be black or Jewish or otherwise conspicuously not just like them.

---

[109] Jerrold M. Packard, *American Nightmare, The History of Jim Crow*, (New York: St. Martins Press, 2002), pp. 80, 123-124.

An early film, based upon a 1905 novel by Woodrow Wilson's college roommate, Thomas Dixon, entitled "The Birth of a Nation" (D.W. Griffith, 1915), was widely viewed and lauded. It portrayed blacks as lazy, idiotic leeches, sympathy-seekers, shoeless, moronic embarrassments, and eulogized white supremacy. The film swept the nation and was highly praised by many of the powerful.[110]

The more fortunate part of the nation enjoyed unprecedented prosperity and high old times in the '20s, followed by the bottom falling out suddenly in 1929, leading to a long, dispiriting Great Depression taking up the whole decade of the '30s.

Then, there came another, even bigger world war, testing and eventually righting the economy in the first half of the '40s.

Such was the turbulent experience of the generation so roundly praised by ex-anchorman and establishment icon Tom Brokaw's best-selling book *The Greatest Generation* (New York: Random House, 1998).

A great many of my readers (if I am, indeed, fortunate enough to *have* many readers) are no doubt asking right now *how on earth* one can even begin to square all of *these horrendous, nonstop departures* by the American nation virtually as whole (that is, *not limited to* that traditional whipping boy, the government) happening *continuously*, generation after generation, from the nation's beginnings until now – with all of the obviously well-intentioned, constructive, "every-day" citizens profiled in Brokaw's book and extremely common among the Americans we all know and love.

In other words, "*Huh?* I thought we Americans had an overwhelmingly decent and positive record of achievement, both at home and around the world. So, where do you get off, trying to suggest otherwise? Look-a-here, sonny boy! Just who do you think you are, anyway?*"

My rejoinder? "*Look at the record!*"

And, peeking ahead, right on down to the present, it only gets *even worse*, if that's possible! So, *brace yourselves*, friends! And consider yourselves warned!"

The fact is, I like and admire as much as anyone the same common and good sorts of people extolled not only by Tom Brokaw, but by *all* of the media sources, endlessly echoed daily from and by nearly everyone around us, every day of our lives.

---

[110] Ibid., pp. 126, 162 ff. Of course, not all white southerners in this lengthy period were supporting the continuation of a state policy of segregation and exclusion. For instance, John T. Kneebone, *Southern Liberal Journalists and the Issue of Race, 1920-1946*, (Chapel Hill: Univ. of North Carolina Press, 1985).

"Americans are good people!" So, how in the world can we square the two seemingly *opposite* types of messages about who we are and how we've done with our values and how we're still doing this very day?

Truthfully, I'm not altogether sure; but I hasten to add: I *do* believe, and don't for a moment discount, the actual historical record that I've been citing here, through several generational chapters.

And, I also have enough respect for the type of good citizens Tom Brokaw extols, and everyone else extols, too, to believe that they (*we, for goodness sake!*) are *capable* of radically and abruptly *correcting* our course in every single aspect of our national life to actually *begin to adhere* to our tremendous and truly exceptional, world-renowned national creed *for the first time ever*, and thus, *fully straighten out our obviously rudderless, wayward country. That's* my hope for an enormously better country and world than we have now in the years ahead!

Let's examine *all* things in terms of our truly great, unsurpassed but unfulfilled, five-part creed. And then, let's make darn sure we're living up to it! And, then, *I guarantee*, we'll see things improve in a big way that will amaze the world!

And, this I say for a reason: because *I don't think the Revolutionary founders of our country, who coined our creed, were simply sentimental fools.* I think they were, in fact, *realists*, harboring in their deep and thoughtful minds the *creedal* notions that we all have memorized by rote and swear by to this day, and that we can also *harness and practice* for true, unrivaled power and wisdom. If we do that, *no one* can stop us! The *only* stumbling block before us is our own resolve.

*   *   *

One of the biggest problems – among a plethora of them – with huge *central banking schemes* with which we've been plagued is, as we've already *seen* plenty of times, that such are eminently *manipulable*.

And, in the case of the so-called Federal Reserve System we are beset with now, the fact that its *charter*, honored in practice, provides it with a veil of secrecy that greatly accentuates the manipulability is because, naturally, no one is watching. And, we all know from experience that the sort of high-octane, genius-class people who wind up in super-powerful positions in government, mega-business, and mega-finance tend to be just a click past eccentric (or *crazy*) and require oversight and, preferably, *transparency*.

In the case of the Fed, back in the '20s, it seems that there was something more than *business affinity* in the air between Benjamin Strong, the head of the flagship Federal Reserve Bank of New York and Montagu Norman, the head of the Bank of England in London, who swore in correspondence that they "must live together sometimes."

According to historian Carroll Quigley, "In the 1920s, they [Strong and Montagu] were determined to use the financial power of Britain and of the United States to force all the major countries of the world to go on the gold standard and to operate through central banks free from political control, with all questions of international finance to be settled by agreements by such central banks without interference from governments."[111]

During the "Roaring Twenties", the Fed made hard money in America a little scarce in order to aid the Bank of England's mission of retaining the gold standard and attractiveness of investment in Britain.

But credit was made very cheap, and the rules governing margin made it easy for anyone to invest *big* and cheaply in instantly profitable stock. And ordinary people followed the high-rolling "Robber Barons" in doing just that, mortgaging their homes and farms to get the money to plunge *big* into the exotic realm of easy-money stocks, and plunge the U.S. into a quagmire of debt – keeping gold-backed money flooding out of Britain and into America. All this artificially stimulated activity created an enormous inflation bubble.

Then, determining that a crash was coming inexorably, the two trans-Atlantic partners sent warnings to their large, preferred clients. They alone knew just when to sell out their stock holdings and then when to re-buy at a depressed price, to make a killing. Everyone else lost shirts, homes, farms, savings, borrowings, businesses, lunch ... and not seldom, leaped to their deaths, in the crash of 1929.[112]

This was, in a sense, the first fruit of the control system the U.S. government had been heavily induced to accept, and which we still live at the whim of – as conclusively shown recently. And, just as then, we *can't snap right out of it*. Still not enough evidence?

But instead of shutting down the scam that transformed the U.S. economy into a gigantic slush fund and prosecuting the miscreant(s), Congress established the FDIC – a federal funds guarantee band-aid in case they did it again!

We (Congress for us, primarily) never seem to learn our lesson, even when the manipulators (our agents) brazenly put in charge almost flippantly risk the

---

[111] Carroll Quigley, *Tragedy and Hope: A History of the World in Our Time*, (New York: Macmillan, 1966), p. 326.

[112] See Ellen Hodgson Brown, op. cit., pp. 143-146. Murray N. Rothbard, op. cit., pp. 271, 508, identifies Benjamin Strong as but an accolade of supremely-powerful banker J.P. Morgan, head of the House of Morgan, "architect of the world depression."

whole of the nation's economic engine, severely compromising both our *personal and national independence* in the process? To say nothing of Congress's willful flaunting of the Constitutional requirement. *Again, how can – how does this happen?*

On a more pleasant note, two members of the United States Senate who determined that too much concentrated ungoverned power was inimical to the public interest, were Joseph M. O'Mahoney of Wyoming and William E. Borah of Idaho. These two lawmakers observed that early in the nation's history, the standard for business *incorporation* had passed from meeting "public purpose" criteria, requiring applicants to show that their business would provide a public benefit, to "general purpose," requiring no such demonstration or benefit.

And, following the money as mighty fortunes accrued, the role of corporation chartering had passed long since from the federal government's function and oversight capability to the states, with the *most-lenient* states attracting the most businesses. (Micro-state Delaware, where applicants simply *write their own* terms of charter, directly profits the most, with more than 50% of the nation's largest five hundred corporations, in operation nationwide and far, far beyond, registered there, but still confronts U.S. law.)

Senators O'Mahoney and Borah resolved to reign in the untrammeled power of big business by re-introducing public purpose chartering, as an inalienable function of the federal government. They submitted legislation to that effect numerous times in the 1930s, and it came closest to passage late in 1941, when even larger events, sadly, derailed it.[113]

As most everyone knows, conservative Republicans resoundingly lost the White House in the 1932 election a couple of years into the Depression. But what not everyone realizes is just how bitter they may have been about it, and about being tagged by their "radical" opposite number and ordinary citizens – except for some holdouts on Main Street – for their clients' perceived part in trashing the economy.

How radical were FDR's views, from a contemporary Republican perspective? "The real truth of the matter," the new, "radical" president wrote in a letter to Colonel Edward House on October 21, 1933, "is, as you and I know, that a financial element in the larger centers has owned the Government since the days of Andrew Jackson."[114]

---

[113] Ellis W. Hawley, *The New Deal and the Problem of Monopoly*, (Princeton, NJ: Princeton Univ. Press, 1971), pp. 371-372. The State of Delaware's power to require restitution or preventative measures to insure against the recurrence of a mega-accident in Bhopal, India, for example, is doubtful.

[114] Cited by Russ Baker, op. cit., p. 1.

Even before this man elected to turn things around – this patrician Democrat Franklin Delano Roosevelt, who had won the public's trust through his assuring rhetoric and demeanor – had taken office, there was an aborted assassination attempt. The perpetrator was, at least ostensibly, a lone gunman, an unemployed Italian Anarchist named Guiseppe Zangara. The attempt – made during a speech by the still president-elect in Miami, Florida, in February 1933 – was quietly foiled and the gunman apprehended.

The news media at the time, oddly, made little of it. There were rumors of involvement by gangland figures. And, again, the similarities between the profiles of the "unaided lone gunman" perpetrators in so many of these assassinations and assassination attempts do at least seem a bit more than strange, pointing prospectively to a larger agenda.

In response to the Depression and collapsed economy, the Fed chose to offer *no* new monetary programs or steps whatsoever to provide a corrective, claiming that the problem was one of production, and *not at all* monetary missteps or misdirection.

In reaction to the Fed's stunning inaction, the government (while still in Republican hands) did not in any way discipline or turn aside from the blame-dodging institution. Instead, the GOP-led government simply established *a new agency*, the Reconstruction Finance Corporation (RFC), originally under President Herbert Hoover, to concentrate revenues and shift money to the ailing banks, after a third of them had already permanently closed their doors.[115]

Much of *FDR's* early economic program to counteract the problems caused primarily to ordinary people by the Depression consisted of a plethora of directed socioeconomic programs, ranging from the Tennessee Valley Authority and Rural Electrification Administration to Social Security and unemployment insurance – altogether, a novel economic program to respond to the needs of *the people who had taken control* by sweeping Roosevelt into office.[116] In addition to the numerous *pro-citizen* programs he did manage to establish during his lengthy tenure, later on, in his 1944 State of the Union speech, President

Roosevelt would call on Congress to pass legislation guaranteeing all citizens a decent and secure income, affordable health services, a chance for a good practices, and prices guaranteeing a decent return for farmers. He called this blockbuster legislative package a *"Second Bill of Rights."* Unfortunately, this initiative ended up getting lost and abandoned in the midst of a flood of

---

[115] Richard H. Timberlake, *Monetary Policy in the United States, An Intellectual and Institutional History*, (Chicago: Univ. of Chicago Press, 1993), p. 275 ff.
[116] Ellen Hodgson Brown, op. cit., pp. 153-154.

end-of-the-war priorities soon to follow, and has been fulfilled only in small part in the years since.[117]

Needless to say, the Wall Street types in particular were infuriated by this unprecedented direct government approach. Reportedly, they tried to nip such patent nonsense in the bud, via a scheme duly reported to authorities by highly-decorated, outspoken retired Marine General Smedley D. Butler.

A respected figure, Smedley Butler had, he alleged, been courted by Wall Street bankers and VFW Veterans of Foreign Wars) officials to lead a 1933/34 military coup and Fascist dictatorship replacing FDR. The results were nil, though the report, although denied by those implicated, was regarded as credible due to Butler putting his reputation on the line to expose it. But no one was prosecuted and no official investigation was ever authorized, suggesting that perhaps much more was known about it on the inside.[118]

In retrospect, the Depression years were not the most honorable for the magisterial central banking cult and its allies in the U.S. Its very survival perhaps bespeaks the lingering power of the green, and possibly of fear of retribution, over lawmakers, even during a period of radical policies and change.

Back in the days before the advent of the notorious racialist eugenics program in Germany, there were the American racialist eugenics studies. These studies, starting in the early twentieth century, led to benchmark principles and selective sterilization laws in a number of states, which Adolf

Hitler admired and emulated, and whose practitioners he actively corresponded with. This is so, even though there have been attempts after the fact to deny it.

Marked similarities between the recommendations and wording of sterilization laws in the United States in the 1930s (and before) and in the German versions under the Nazis have been pointed to by a consensus of interested historians.[119]

The relationship of German scientists to treatment of the Jews in Germany during the 1930s was outrageously (by current standards) compared by apologists in America seeking justification at the time to that of American

---

[117] See Cass R. Sunstein, *The Second Bill of Rights*, (New York: Basic Books, 2004).

[118] Hans Schmidt, *Maverick Marine, General Smedley D. Butler, and the Contradictions of American Military History*, (Lexington: Univ. of Kentucky Press, 1987), pp. 222-226. Notably, fascism didn't yet carry the discredited reputation in the U.S. it gained later.

[119] Stephen Kühl, *The Nazi Connection, Eugenics, American Racism, and German National Socialism*, (New York: Oxford Univ. Press, 1994), pp. xiv-xv.

scientists, by and large, *vis-à-vis* blacks in the United States. Richard Goldschmidt, an American anthropologist who began as an immigrant from Germany, even argued that German scientists and Nazis, unlike in the American case, were deluded in the desire to keep their dominant national population pure of unclean elements, through the weapon of sterilization.

This was because both the Jews and general German populations were products of a mixture of genetic elements and indistinguishable on that score – unlike the two populations viewed in America.

Eugenicist Madison Grant was lauded by several prominent colleagues in the early 1930s for entering the immigration debate by voicing "opposition to the flooding of this country [the U.S.] with alien scum."

American researcher Elizar Barkan described "Jewishness" as physically determined, noting the supposed "Jewish nose." A colleague, Earnest Hooton, said, referring to Jews, geneticists must "strive to eradicate certain aggressive and other social characteristics" that "account for some of their trouble."[120]

"Differential Fertility" was code used by Frederick Osborn and other eugenicists for the decried decline of white American stock, supposedly alarmingly out-bred by genetically inferior populations. American geneticist Osborn praised the Nazi eugenics program in 1937 as the "most important experiment that has ever been tried", and called their sterilization program "apparently an excellent one."[121]

A large number of U.S. states already had judicially operated sterilization programs on the books, arbitrarily targeting "genetically weaker" individuals and, by emphasis, groups by the 1920s and in some cases before, and in the 1930s, the eugenicists were attempting to validate and adjust these measures scientifically to enhance their benefit and effectiveness. Thus, when Hitler came along, he looked to what had come to be known as American racialist science and its practitioners as a primary source for answers and guidance.[122]

A question worth asking is, how would (*did*) *selective* internment in camps of U.S. citizens square with the American national creed?

The details are murky, perhaps purposefully so, but a prominent Wall Street banking firm, the Brown Brothers Harriman group – one of whose associates was named *Prescott Bush* – had assets seized by the U.S. government in the midst of World War II for continuing business operations

---

[120] Ibid., pp. 60-61, 80.

[121] Ibid., p. 75, citing Frederick Olmsted, "Summary of the Proceedings of the Conference on Eugenics in Relation to Nursing," February 24, 1937, *American Eugenics Society Papers*.

[122] Edwin Black, *War Against the Weak, Eugenics and America's Campaign to Create a Master Race*, (New York: Thunder's Mouth Press, 2003), pp. 87 ff, 279 ff.

(not impossibly in the company of others known to have been like-minded) with top German industrialists at a time when they were financing Hitler and the rise of Naziism.[123]

Unacknowledged as it generally is, the "greatest generation" that defeated tyranny overseas was still officially and unofficially bigoted and oppressive at home. Sadly, one is left wondering what *were* the *American values* they thought they were fighting for?

Army Captain Harold Montgomery, who had led a heavy weapons company of the 92nd 'Buffalo Soldiers' Infantry Division against withering German fire up the west coast of Italy, arrived back home in Washington, D.C., after a 4-1/2 years' absence after the Allied victory was won. Returning to reclaim his old job and passing through the high-ceilinged lobby at the GAO headquarters, he looked for his name on the big plaque honoring Postal Department employees who had served – and found there *no names of blacks included*. Nor was any returning black soldier offered the pay raise given to returning white soldiers. He walked away and looked, in vain, for a more receptive new job in still-segregated, repressive America. *A creed that is empty is meaningless*. Montgomery reports he stayed angry for years.[124]

---

[123] Russ Baker, *Family of Secrets, The Bush Dynasty, The Powerful Forces That Put It In the White House, and What Their Influence Means for America*, (New York: Bloomsbury Press, 2009), p. 17; Kevin Philips, *American Dynasty*, (New York: Penguin, 2004), pp. 19-20.

[124] Nurith C. Aizenman, *Washington Post*, May 26, 2001, p. B01. A question currently posed is: can minority Americans be faulted if they don't return the embrace?

Part 9 – **Running Ahead** – 1945 to 1967

Late in 1945, the Nuremburg international war crimes trial convened. Its purpose was not to wreak vengeance, but instead to bring the fullest possible measure of justice against those German Nazi officials still alive, who had been charged with willfully causing deaths by the million (an estimated 35 million) of their fellow human beings, plus the displacement of millions of others, and the partial or near-total material destruction of several countries of Europe and North Africa. Notably, the penalty sought was not against the German nation. Salt was not sown in its fields, nor slavery imposed in this instance, nor the razing of any more cities.

Of equal note as a precedent for state crimes or misfeasance: there was not an authoritative call to *just let what was in the past be in the past*, untouched by inquiry or sanction, and just move on to the future. Instead, the standard sought was *justice*. Not political vindication or reconciliation. *Justice*.

Hitler was beyond human justice. But, if he had remained alive, he would have been taken to Nuremburg and interrogated and justice served. The denial or impeding of *justice*, on whatever grounds, would have been seen, rightly, as complicity.[125]

General Dwight Eisenhower, at the end of the war, showed himself to be more than a tool of politicians or politics, of whatever stripe. He ordered extensive filming of the gruesome victims and carnage of the massive Nazi death camp discovered by his armies' final advance, and ordered people from the surrounding countryside to view and even to work in the task of mass burial, to create a record and witnesses of the overwhelming sights, smells, sounds of unspeakable horror. Thus, his thinking ran, no one *ever* could plausibly deny the truth of the atrocity and its magnitude – a matter beyond ideology. Eisenhower himself would not be the same afterward.[126]

President Roosevelt exceeded President Wilson's success by getting what was ostensibly his grand League of Nations project approved with United States participation. But, the plan, as ratified, was not on the Jeffersonian/*creedal* model of equal democracy among nations. As it happened, the powers in control of Congress would accede to a plan only with a powerful U.S. veto on the decisions rendered by a majority, lacking a direct means of gaining revenue for its operations, and with limited actual powers.

---

[125] See William E. Shapiro, ed., _Trial at Nuremburg_, (New York: CBS, 1967).
[126] Remembrance of Andrew Rosner, surviving prisoner of the Ohrdraf Nazi Concentration Camp, at a ceremony to honor the 89th Infantry Division of the U.S. Army on the fiftieth anniversary of its liberation of the camp, at Wichita, KS, on April 23, 1995.

Still, it did provide a forum, and the other nations that comprise over 95% of the world's people have proven on occasion that they can't always be goaded into voting as the dominant nation or nations (for instance, the Anglo-American alliance from the late great war) desire or dictate.

Significantly, paired with the withholding of a truly democratic world structure, was an act of considerable – but perhaps deceptive to a great extent – largess called the "Marshall Plan". Under the Truman administration, immediately succeeding FDR's, the U.S. – the only rich Western country to survive the war materially intact – commanded the unconditional support of the war-torn nations on both sides in Europe, plus ravaged Japan, by footing the bill for their reconstruction. (Substituting *benefits for power* to silence dissenters is as old as the proverbial "bread and circuses" under the Romans.)

In the meantime, help with economic construction was requested by the much poorer, non-Western countries wanting desperately to reduce the great gap between themselves and the powerful countries, which had until that moment kept most of them in imperial bondage. Viewed as of lesser importance, their needs were approached differently.

The International Monetary Fund and the World Bank – set up ostensibly to aid the poorer great majority of nations through loans from the rich countries' dominant banking systems – in fact burdened them with exploitative loans, juiced with adjustable rates, that, in nearly every instance, kept the poor countries – home to a growing majority of the world's people – dependent and economically strapped.

Hence, they were effectively prevented from realizing their outstanding potential for development and true independence. The result has been that absolutely no whole, genuine country *anywhere* that wasn't industrially developed before the end of World War II has ever broken free to become a developed country, down to the present day. *Why?*

Fairly obviously: because the controlling investor and corporate elite financiers have so deemed. The poor countries' bargain basement labor and raw materials are just too convenient and lucrative to give up. To say nothing of the enormous profits made by major "first world" enterprises for providing virtually all of the value-adding processing and manufacturing components on the path to phenomenal retail mark-ups that the poor lack the wherewithal to perform. Because, those factors are exactly what keep the rich in the world so VERY rich.

Obviously, *so much* can't be given up just to give the poor *billions* of the world a life! Hence, friendly, low-cost, non-profit, *manageable* loans – or just no-strings-attached aid and perhaps a share of real power on this planet we all share, none more so than another – have remained out of the question. And, many get mad when some of the other 95% don't *jump into line* for us!

*   *   *

Except for participation in archaeological digs and the like that extend back decades further, American (not to say Western) involvement in the Middle East dates to the early 1930s.[127] At the time, some American oil companies negotiated concessions in the Kingdom of Saudi Arabia. These were forerunners of ARAMCO, the highly lucrative Arabian-American oil consortium and source of many lasting ties of business and friendship.

At the end of World War II, it was recognized that the old, paternalistic and exploitative national empires of Europe could no longer maintain economically viable control over far-flung families of colonies as in the past. They would have to set free their increasingly tenuous control over their many remaining colonial dependencies, primarily in the Middle East, elsewhere in Asia, in the Caribbean, and in Africa, at least on paper. Thus, the French and British colonies in North, Central, and Southern Africa were gradually released by the Western colonialist powers, as were India and Indonesia, smaller Caribbean Islands and, reluctantly, Malaya, Indo-China, and the half-century old American chokehold on the Philippines. Israel was created, partly under American auspices, in the former mandated territory of Palestine.

Especially after the British and French lost their joint control over the super-strategic Suez Canal to Egypt a few years later, American resolve heightened to replace those two powers as the kingpin in the region, in partnership with embattled Israel.

Meanwhile, Arab resistance to growing Jewish-American hegemony over their region grew and festered. And, after a decades-long Soviet bid for a role in the Middle East flamed out, the U.S.-Israeli partnership grew to be even more about strategic intelligence and defensive control by any means necessary. But, in the 1950s, most of that was still in the future.

As has been the case with other American wars, both before and since, the official version of the start and provocation of the Korean War of the early 1950s, designed to gain public support for the war effort, bore scarce resemblance to the later-verified truth of what took place.

In this case, it was stated to the world that units of the North Korean armed forces staged a completely unexpected surprise attack on South Korean forces. It was subsequently learned, and eventually admitted, that the North Koreans, seeking to bring about reunification of the peninsula, a region with a single population, marched peacefully south beyond the 38th parallel, ostensibly in hopes that the people of the south would fall in behind them and produce a *de facto* unification that the leaders on both sides would be obliged to negotiate the means to honor and preserve. But, the result instead was that

---

[127] King Saud, the Saudi monarch at the time, once said that he selected the Americans to partner with because they knew the oil business, just as the other bidding countries did, and were also much farther away.

the South Korean army mounted forays during the night on June 25, 1950, against the advancing column of North Korean troops and commenced the war.

It was later confirmed as well that the North Korean units had been amassing in the vicinity of the provisional border for some time, pretty clearly in view of observers to the south, so their movement forward *could not* have come as much of a surprise.

Nevertheless, the American and British ambassadors at the UN Security Council moved to have North Korea declared the aggressor, although the Council report (and that issued to the U.S. Congress as well) deleted – *substituting dots* – the four words "on basis this evidence," originally a qualifier in the report. This was apparently because available evidence, if actually consulted, would have indicated otherwise. The Council's final report stated in summary: "All the evidence continues to point to a calculated coordinated attack prepared and launched with secrecy," *without citing specifics.*

In the days leading up to the start of the war, the Truman administration's secretary of state, Acheson, and the administration's legislative leader in Congress, Senator Tom Conolly, spoke equivocally with regard to the U.S. standing by South Korea in case of an attack from the North. In Conolly's case, averring that a Communist takeover of the entire peninsula might be inevitable, and that South Korea wasn't essential to the Pacific Defense Perimeter protecting Japan.

John Foster Dulles, the State Department's Republican advisor, spoke in what were called "Cold War generalities" in addressing the South Korean Assembly days before the war began.[128]

The U.S. did honor its commitment, along with allies, to stand with the South Koreans – even in deceit. In the end, the pragmatic mutual realization that neither side – neither the North Koreans with their Chinese allies and Russian suppliers, nor the South Koreans with American and Western allies –

---

[128] I.F. Stone, *The Hidden History of the Korean War, 1950-1951* [1952], (Boston: Little, Brown, 1988), pp. 1 ff, 12 ff, 44-45, 49-50. It may have been that the North Koreans refused to fire the first shot, while fully realizing that their presence was certain to provoke an attack. Historian I.F. Stone wondered why it was that the Republicans in Congress had not demanded an investigation of the reported attack by the North Koreans, as they had in the case of Pearl Harbor, nine years earlier (which later turned out probably not to have been a total surprise as portrayed at the time). Stone reported a year later that the intelligence of General MacArthur, Commander of the Pacific Theater, had inadvertently admitted that MacArthur had lied in reporting to Congress on the North Korean "attack". See p. 57; See also Robert Stinnett, Day of Deceit, *The Truth About FDR and Pearl Harbor*, (New York: Free Press, 2001).

could fulfill its objective, led to a stalemate. A negotiation – even based on the North's charade – would have done as well, saving blood and treasure.

In *Plessy v. Fergusson* (1896), the U.S. Supreme Court had upheld the practice of racial segregation, by affirming the doctrine of "separate but equal." In *Oliver Brown, et al v. Board of Education of Topeka* (1954), the Court under Chief Justice Earl Warren (appointed by Eisenhower), definitively overturned the earlier ruling at least in the realm of public education. (The Court ruled that *Plessy v. Fergusson* didn't apply as a precedent, because that case involved transportation, not education.) In December 1953, finding itself strangely unable – after reviewing six months' worth of staff research – to determine whether or not Congress, in passing the 14th Amendment after the Civil War, had intended to outlaw or approve segregated schools, the Court ruled essentially on the question posed by future Justice Thurgood Marshall of whether the Constitution would favor the southern states' efforts to keep blacks as close to the status of slaves as the destruction of slavery would allow. The consensus was that its intent was, at least, not that.

For the very first time, *Brown v. Board of Education* applied the equality clause of the 14th Amendment to the lives and rights of black people, honoring the purpose that had occasioned its adoption in the first place – rather than evasively deferring its language to advantage at least questionable business practices, the mischievous reasoning that had frequently been employed to perversely bolster black *inequality* – manifestly *not* what had been intended by the so-called "radical amendment."[129]

The results of the 1954 ruling were both immediate and far-reaching. The ordered desegregation of Little Rock Central High School that year produced a violent clash, as, famously, did school desegregations elsewhere in the South and not infrequently in the North. The white segregationist South rose up in arms – in some instances, literally.

Throughout the nation, ordered bussing of students as a remedy to achieve racial balance was largely opposed. Public schools throughout the South became black schools exclusively, as families in droves enrolled their children in new, "all-white" private schools to avoid integration. Calls rang out across America for Chief Justice Warren's head.

On the other hand, having been handed a giant victory by the Supreme Court in this instance, American blacks, wanting the much ballyhooed *creedal* tenets of *"All men (persons) are created equal"* and *"Liberty and justice for all"* affirmed, including outlawing discrimination in every possible aspect of life, revived and expanded the Civil Rights Movement.

---

[129] Peter Irons, op. cit., pp. 391 ff.

Less directly perhaps, white college-age students were impressed by this overturn by the Court of what they, too, perceived as a hidebound institution and inequitable "solution" that were in fact outrageous and ugly stains on the spirit and practice of America's creed.

From this perceived victory, they gathered impetus for the beginnings of a loosely strung companion movement protesting, mocking, and challenging all perceived social limitations and unfair practices in the years ahead. Which, in turn, led to powerful, positively revengeful *pro-authority* decades of counter-surge from the right. Thus, the unmatched *Sixties* rumbled into vivid view.

Aside from the Korean War and the darkening intrigue of the building Cold War, a match of wits for world hegemony against the Communist Eastern Bloc led by the Soviets, the decade of the 1950s was a deceptively placid and prosperous one on the surface, with powerful and treacherous currents running deep.

The CIA (Central Intelligence Agency), successor to the wartime OSS (Office of Strategic Services) was founded in 1947, as the counterpart of clandestine and unaccountable Soviet intelligence, the extending device of what was later termed "the evil empire."

As one scholar has stated, "Certain elements in the domestic side of the Cold War imaginary [sic] displayed an uncomfortable similarity to elements of the Soviet regime: purges, loyalty tests, violations of due process, criminalization of a political party for its beliefs rather than its actions, development of an elaborate, largely secretive agency with a global network of spies and assassins (CIA) dedicated to subverting regimes deemed unfriendly or uncooperative and installing sympathetic ones."

A study group reporting to President Eisenhower urged explicitly that the United not only follow the Soviet example but seek to surpass it."[130]

"We are facing," read the report of this very study group, "an implacable enemy whose avowed object is world domination by whatever means and at whatever cost. [T]here are no rules in such a game."[131]

According to many, the CIA outdid the Soviet apparatus, its model, at projecting globally the principles of its founders. President Harry Truman lamented, years later (in 1961), "I never would have agreed to the formation of the CIA back in '47, if I had known it would become the American Gestapo."[132]

---

[130] Sheldon S. Wolin, *Democracy Incorporated*, (Princeton, NJ: Princeton Univ. Press, 2008), p. 36.

[131] Stephen J. Whitfield, *The Culture of the Cold War*, (Baltimore: Johns Hopkins Univ. Press, 1996), p. 34.

[132] Quoted in David Barnet, *The CIA and Congress, The Untold Story from Truman to Kennedy*, (Lawrence: Univ. of Kansas Press, 2005).

One of the CIA's first major targeted victims was the fiercely independent Mohammed Mosaddegh, the popular elected prime minister of Iran, overthrown in a staged rebellion for not playing ball. Reportedly, the act, in 1953, was performed at the request of MI6, British Intelligence. The favor would be returned.

The stupendous Cold War buildup of arms and exports of arms, past a point of superfluous excess, had an even greater purpose beyond protection and deterrence. That purpose was obscene profits for the big investors whose donations kept both major political parties in the U.S. afloat, but especially the usually more reliable Republicans. These same investors – many of them living in congressional districts with major military bases, defense contractors, and lots of veterans – definitely had a thing going.

And they must have been aghast when, at the end of his active service at their presumed beck and call, retiring President Dwight Eisenhower showed again that he wasn't to be bought. The country's fatherly president and foremost hero of "the good war" (World War II) warned America in his televised "Farewell Address," on January 17, 1961, of its most dangerous clear and present danger. (His model apparently was President Washington's 1797 "Farewell Address," which warned similarly against "foreign entanglements.")

"In the councils of government," he memorably intoned, "we must guard against the acquisition of unwarranted influence, whether sought or unsought, by the military industrial complex. The potential for the disastrous rise of misplaced power exists and will persist. We must never let the weight of this combination endanger our liberties or democratic processes... so that security and liberty may prosper together." And we can only conclude that he may have *understated* the wiliness of this supreme foe.

The Platt Amendment, under which the U.S. had dictated Cuban affairs since the beginning of the twentieth century, was finally replaced under FDR in 1934 by a "Treaty of Relations," which abrogated the conditions of the special guardianship, except for reconfirming U.S. occupation of Guantanamo Bay (supposedly until 1997).

Still, a succession of Cuban leaders continued to serve essentially as U.S. puppets and benefactors of American business interests, a situation resented by the people of Cuba as much as U.S. blacks resented their state-enforced subordination to whites.

At the end of the decade of the '50s, the wildly popular local insurgent leader Fidel Castro managed to oust by force of arms the U.S. puppet dictator Batista and become the independent head of state of Cuba. He put out feelers to the American government at once, seeking a working accord on the basis of mutuality and respect, as Haiti's revolutionary leader Toussaint L'Ouverture, had once done in vain.

But, his overtures were similarly met with haughty suspicion and dismissed. Soon, plans were afoot for re-invasion or subversion, to restore a government the U.S. could control. Castro then turned to the congratulatory Soviet Union for military and later economic help, not by choice, but of necessity to safeguard the interests of ordinary Cubans.

Rather amazingly, Castro, the popular folk hero leader of lowly Cuba, was converted into a Cold War bogeyman and figure of loathing.[133]

The new president who took office only days after Eisenhower's "Farewell Address" John F. Kennedy, was also a Cold Warrior. But his sense of America's true needs, our failure to date at living up to the hopes and promises of its Founders, and of his own capacity to do some of the fulfilling, made him a worthy bearer of the mantle of champion and protector. He was intelligent and elegant, stylish, a man of wit, a quick study of what was essential that he didn't previously know. He wanted to make his country better.

He received and worked with the great civil rights leader Rev. Martin Luther King, Jr. as a colleague, reminiscent of the way President Lincoln had received and worked with Frederick Douglass and continued learning and growing while he was in the White House.

He managed foreign policy with an increasingly deft hand, learning from some glaring mistakes as he progressed. America's two great bugaboos of the period, the unmanageable Castro regime in Cuba and the perceived Soviet nuclear threat, merged in the deadly "Cuban missile crisis" of 1962. But, in that heart-stopping sequence, the president's performance made his administration's failure in the so-called Bay of Pigs fiasco in 1961 – a matter about which he had misgivings from the start – pale into insignificance.

But Kennedy's military advisors continued to fear the advance of international Communism, as well as smart at the seeming Road Runner-like survival of Fidel Castro, still at the helm in Cuba despite their fervent intentions to the contrary.

A team headed by Chairman of the Joint Chiefs of Staff, General Lyman Lemnitzer, came to President Kennedy by mid-1962 with a joint military intelligence-CIA plan called Operation Northwoods, calling for a false-flag, terror op, shoot-down of a U.S. airliner in the vicinity of Cuban airspace and

---

[133] Popular except to the rich, who couldn't face sharing power. Why didn't Castro ever consent to putting himself before his fellow Cubans in a free and open election? Getting ahead of ourselves: what happened when the Nicaraguan revolutionary leader Daniel Ortega did that may be instructive. In that election in the 1980s, the CIA quietly filtered a reported $13 million – an impossible sum by Nicaraguan standards – to Ortega's opponent to practically monopolize the airwaves and dictate his downfall – something that bullets and airstrikes and harbor mining had been unable to bring about. Ortega came back later and returned to office by popular vote.

blaming Cuba. The objective would be to create enough anger in the American populace to guarantee support for an invasion. JFK said flat-out, "No."[134]

Who assassinated Kennedy on November 22, 1963, and why? The American public remains unsatisfied by the Warren Commission's recitation of the usual "lone gunman" explanation in answer to those questions, which doesn't seem to fit the evidence. Consequently, theories abound. One of the more compelling and chilling possibilities is cogently suggested by journalist Russ Baker.[135]

Increasingly, scholars of the pivotal assassination are concluding that domestic foes, powerful enough to commandeer inside cooperation, must have been responsible. For one thing, Kennedy wanted to promote our *independence* by developing cheap alternative energy sources, while the oil/banking cartel sought to drastically raise oil prices to ensnare the world in debt. He also sought to revive the concept of a silver-backed currency independent of the Federal Reserve structure. This plan wasn't fully operationalized, but he authorized the Treasury to issue silver certificates, and was the last to emit freely-circulating United States Notes (called "Greenbacks").[136]

Kennedy's foreign policy sought to end the exploitative perpetual dependence and relegation to mere exporting of raw materials that degraded the prospects of virtually all non-Western countries. After learning of Operation Northwoods, he planned to strip the CIA of its covert operations capability.

It now appears that such advances, bringing us in sync with principles of our national *creed*, might be achieved only through persistent, unrelenting, overwhelming popular demand, to be maintained by the kind of eternal vigilance called for by Jefferson.[137]

---

[134] The record shows that, as Kennedy's short presidency proceeded, he became more inclined to engage the Soviets on the path to weapons reductions than to challenge and threaten them. Operation Northwoods was classified top secret until 1997. L. James Binder's biography, Lemnitzer, (Washington: Brassey's, 1997), offers neither mention nor clue, except that, after Bay of Pigs, Kennedy ordered continued "sabotage, propaganda, and political action" (p. 259). But, the clear precedent of a plan for the sacrifice of multiples of Americans to achieve an objective exists.

[135] Russ Baker, *Family of Secrets*, op. cit., p. 44 ff.

[136] Interestingly, one of Lyndon Johnson's first official acts as president was to restore Federal Reserve notes. See Donald Gibson, *Battling Wall Street: The Kennedy Presidency*, (New York: Sheridan Square Books, 1994), pp. 41, 79, Ch. 6; Ellen Hodgson Brown, op. cit., p. 206.

[137] Ellen Hodgson Brown, op. cit., p. 207, citing James Bamford, *Body of Secrets, Anatomy of the Ultra-Secret National Security Agency*, (New York: Anchor, 2002).

Assassinations became epidemic in the '60s, always reported as the work of a single "lone gunman" seemingly custom-ordered for the role right out of Central Casting. With a cameraman, it seems, always conveniently present and at the ready to document the apparent, visible action for the folks.[138]

The "domino theory," used to justify America's entry into and staged escalation of the Vietnam War, ultimately spilled over into neighboring Cambodia and Laos, in the 1960s, and tipped over into the '70s. This most simplistic of "theories" or doctrines originated in a memo to the president from the National Security Council in 1950. The idea was that, if Country A fell to Communism, Country B next door was virtually a synch to fall also, and Country C, next to Country B, etc., etc.

With that notion in mind (and dead-set against losing *all those countries*), the United States was quietly footing 80% of the bill for France's war to reassert control of its three-part Indo-China colony by defeating an aggressive independence movement, the indigenous "Communist" Viet Minh.

After the French withdrew from the struggle, the U.S. began to insert advisors and aid under Kennedy, for the non-Communist fledgling government in the south of the country, fighting to remain free of control by the Communist north and the homegrown Communist movement in the south, the Viet Cong.

Under President Johnson, U.S. involvement and aid increased dramatically, and the difficulties of successfully fighting a massive guerrilla insurgency in a distant and utterly foreign tropical environment mounted. The "domino theory," which proved to be quite false, came to be replaced over time by the curious argument that American credibility gave U.S. forces, with a few allies, receiving and inflicting increasingly heavy casualties and losing ground, no choice but to persevere.

It's curious in retrospect that the pro-war "Hawks" never insisted on applying the same imperative to continue to avoid defeat and loss of credibility in the government's "war on poverty" or efforts to achieve energy independence – objectives that would have made a positive difference in people's lives.

But, the really amazing thing is that, with the media cheerleading, an overwhelming, though declining, majority of the public bought the government's argument about the patriotic necessity of persevering to defeat the Communists for several years. It was the military draft that eventually turned the tide at home.[139]

---

[138] See William F. Pepper, *An Act of State, The Execution of Martin Luther King*, (London: Verso, 2008.

[139] Howard Zinn, op. cit., p. 162; Maurice Isserman and Michael Kazin, *America Divided, The Civil War of the 1960s*, (Oxford: Oxford Univ. Press, 2000), p. 67 ff.

In the twenty-nine years immediately following the end of World War II, 57.29% of the federal budget ($904 billion) was spent for military purposes, while a total of $96 billion (6.08%) was spent for what were called "social functions," including education, health, welfare, labor, housing, job training, food programs, etc. The military-industrial complex was already quite persuasive, mostly financed by interest-bearing loans requiring increasing international borrowing.[140]

The Great Society programs of the Johnson Administration might have mitigated the constant sacrifices of money and, especially, lives to the never less than mysterious war – except that, how can death and a needless heavy burden of expense for *who knows what* be mitigated? Once again, though, the mavens of power and control may have been attempting to buy off relinquishment of control with material favors and payouts to the affected clientele, the American public.

The Voting Rights Act of 1964 in particular, while certainly salutary and very much in line with the American *creed*, no doubt did purchase the seriously needed loyalty of a major segment of the military and military-eligible population. This was so even as the measure spelled serious trouble for the Democrats in loss of dedicated *anti-equality* voters and whole regions going forward.

Thus, gains and apparent gains pertaining to the *equality* and *justice* tenets of the national creed were – *perversely* – somewhat offset by major losses regarding the *democratic control, rejection of mandatory government control*, and *national independence* tenets.

America limped forward, is all we can say. The invisible forces that had consolidated control – more quickly and thoroughly than Ike or *anybody* expected – were *in no wise* dislodged or unmanageably challenged, as the advancing "free world" marched on.

The so-called "Tonkin Gulf incident" – a supposed attack on a U.S. ship that precipitated direct U.S. involvement in the Southeast Asia War – was later admitted to have been fabricated, and never really to have happened. For instance, see Myra MacPherson, *Long Time Passing, Vietnam and the Haunted Generation*, (Garden City, NY: Doubleday, 1984), pp. 118, 197, 415, 476.

[140] Sidney Lens, *The Military-Industrial Complex*, (Philadelphia: Pilgrim Press, 1970), p. 1.

Part 10 – Boomers Come of Age – 1968 to 1992

On the face of it, Richard Nixon – with his penchant for secrecy and clandestine trickery, a misfit anxious for top-level approval and acceptance – seems a perfect candidate for wholly owned visible asset of the military-industrial complex so familiar and feared of late by his Republican predecessor. In the end he was perhaps too tight a fit, too much in character. So they dumped him, ruing the association.

As speculation, President Lyndon Johnson, his predecessor, may have acted as he did – relating to the quirky Israeli attack on the *USS Liberty* and then in escalating out-of-control U.S. involvement in the Vietnam War, with its huge implications for financial coffers, armaments, and a hundred other interests – in good part as a response to the tragic result of his predecessor's independence.

The eventual precipitous downfall of Nixon may have involved the lately installed exercisers of American sovereignty's impatience with his failure to bring about an orderly and satisfactory exit after the Indochina War had become unsustainable. The objective at that time, after all, was not the breakdown of American society, clearly under way.

Domestically, neither Nixon, who was repulsed by the spread of grassroots democratic power under his feet, nor *his* handpicked Republican successor, Gerald R. Ford, dared even repudiate the decidedly un-Republican social reforms people had become accustomed to and benefitted from, thanks to the preceding Democratic administrations. The role of dismantling, thereby, fell to the next, more doctrinaire round of Republican presidents.

More than hinting at the total lack of sincerity of successive American administrations regarding the *creedal* sentiment that "*All men (all people*, not just Americans) *are created equal*," Eisenhower's secretary of state, the didactic John Foster Dulles, reportedly once convened a meeting of all the ambassadors of the numerous Latin American countries in Washington to clarify some mandates regarding their area of the world. Entering the conference room, he shook no one's hand, read his communiqué, and left, fielding no discussion or comments. *We speak, you jump.*

On another occasion, the ambassador of Brazil, a country the size of the United States or Europe, read in a newspaper en route the results of a meeting with administration figures before he had arrived to attend it. Stunned, he told his driver to turn around and sent a consular official to attend.

In keeping with this autocratic stance, Secretary Dulles, in 1958, summed up Latin America's problems as one: to fight Communism (meaning arms sales, military subordination and heightened control).

The assumed right of the U.S. to dictate other nations, especially outside the key European circle of allies, was general and palpable. Resisters to U.S. wishes, particularly among lower- or middle-echelon nations, were considered suspect and targets.

The CIA sponsored and helped pay for organized death squads to enforce "national security" orthodoxy throughout Latin America in the 1960s and '70s. These were manned by the 61,000 police and soldiers who were graduates of the School of the Americas at Fort Benning, Georgia, and imposed a pattern of enforced internal order all too familiar from Latin America's violent *caudillo* (local boss) era.[141]

As American casualties in Vietnam mounted to well over 50,000 killed and several times that many injured grievously or left psychologically traumatized for life – to say nothing of the millions of non-American casualties and the threat of the draft to virtually all American young men – the anti-war movement picked up steam by the early '70s. Its proponents in Congress – led by such senators as Wayne Morse, Ernest Gruening, J. William Fullbright, Frank Church, George McGovern, and Mike Gravel, and such representatives as Pete McClosky – slowly gained the upper hand, pushing the Nixon administration to agree to U.S. withdrawal and "Vietnamization" of the war.

The only remaining question was *when*, as the incident at Kent State, in which the Ohio National Guard fired on protesting students, who they were conditioned to view as the enemy, brought a latent surge of public opinion in favor of withdrawal from Southeast Asia.

The real, final end of the war, though – not well known and almost never mentioned in this country – came when resistance to orders became epidemic among U.S. soldiers in Vietnam, as shown in the film, "*Sir, No Sir!*"

After the Watergate affair, the sleazy pretext used by the establishment to remove Nixon from the presidency, the Democratic leaders in Congress who had opposed the war and a belligerent U.S. presence overseas, led by Senator Frank Church of Idaho, felt compelled to investigate and clarify the activities of the main units of U.S. intelligence, especially including the FBI and the super-secretive CIA.

---

[141] Moniz Bandeira, *Presença dos Estados Unidos no Brasil*, (Rio de Janeiro: Civilização Brasileira, 1978), pp. 377-378, 383; Edward S. Herman, *The Real Terror Networks, Terrorism in Fact and Propaganda*, (Boston: South End Press, 1982), p. 110 ff.

Issued amid a fierce rightwing backlash that held efforts to reveal the worst activities of America's security agencies as treasonous and subsequently limit their actions, the Church Committee's report in 1976 forbade spying on American citizens and use of assassination.

President Kennedy had tried to subjugate the CIA to normal governmental control, an effort perhaps contributing to his demise. Now, thanks to the Church Committee, some of the CIA's worst abuses had been revealed, and some, partly due to an almost total lack of executive branch cooperation, had not been.

To begin a build-back of the Central Intelligence Agency to its darkest, ostensibly most resourceful glory days self, after the unwelcome and unseemly probing by Church's Senate inquisition, President Ford, no doubt urged by his shadow masters – those wielding unaccountable power in the background – appointed the rather mysterious George H.W. Bush as the new Director.[142]

Two of the most egregious CIA clandestine programs that escaped in-depth exposure and scrutiny at the time were Operations Gladio and Mockingbird. Operation Gladio was a Cold War plan launched by the CIA in the late 1960s and early '70s to counter the feared influence of the legal – and, to an alarming extent, successful – Communist parties in Western European countries. The idea, it was revealed later, was to arrange to station NATO paramilitary units inconspicuously in the different countries as a foil against feared Communist insurgencies. In practice, the units would cooperate with local right-wing militants to stage false-flag kidnappings, murders, and property attacks to be blamed on Communist insurgent groups (or "gangs") such as the "Red Brigades" and "Baader-Meinhof in order to inflame public opinion against the left.

It turned out, as revealed by independent investigators years later, that the notorious kidnapping and murder blamed on the leftist gangs in 1972 of Italian Prime Minister Aldo Moro, a national leader who strove to forge an independent course, was in reality a false-flag operation of this kind. Moro's brutal murder shocked Europe. It probably had the intended effect at the time, the truth coming out only when the Cold War was no more than a bad dream.[143]

---

[142] Kathryn S. Olmsted, *Challenging the Secret Government*, (Chapel Hill: Univ. of North Carolina Press, 1996), pp. 81-110; Russ Baker, op. cit., p. 259; L. Fletcher Prouty, *The Secret Team, The CIA and Its Allies in Control of the U.S. and the World*, (New York: Skyhorse, 2008), pp. 111 ff.

[143] See Danielle Ganser, *Nato's Secret Armies, Operation Gladio and Terrorism in Western Europe*, (London: Frank Cass, 2005).

The CIA's Operation Mockingbird (not to be confused with "Project Mockingbird", a much less-extensive and less-damaging venture) dates probably from around 1950. Frank Wisner, an undercover official at the State Department, who was assigned to the Foreign Service, signed up students abroad to act as agents for his Office of Policy Coordination. He hired Philip Graham, a graduate of the Army Intelligence School, and publisher of the *Washington Post* to direct his propaganda program.

A decade later, both Wisner and Graham left the CIA via "suicide." Philip Graham's widow, Katherine Graham, recalled in an interview for a biography of her by Deborah Davis that "Wisner had implemented his plan and 'owned' respected members of the *New York Times, Newsweek, CBS,* and other communications vehicles, plus stringers, four to six hundred in all, according to a former CIA analyst."

Allen Dulles, brother of John Foster Dulles, Eisenhower's secretary of state, oversaw the entire operation as CIA Director, as it mushroomed to represent exclusively the interests and point of view in the media of American and German corporations and to embrace the whole of what is now referred to as the "mainstream media," rendering the idea of a free press in America just one more ballyhooed myth, the ubiquitous, systematic maintenance of which is one of our more preposterous public lies.[144]

Jimmy Carter, as president, served the twin causes of peace and fairness by negotiating the Camp David Accords (1978) between Israel and Egypt, the closest any American administration – *or anyone else* – has come to brokering an end to the many-decades-long standoff in the Middle East. Unfortunately the powers-that-be that strictly hem in every U.S. president wouldn't permit Carter's characteristic largess to reach out so far as to make amends with independent-tending Iran, still justly bitter over the CIA-engineered coup there in the 1950s.

And so, Carter and America had to pay for the behind-the-scenes oligarchy's intransigence – aided by the scheming retinue of Carter's successor.

The hapless Carter's successor, Ronald Reagan, in repudiating the social compact of the government directly benefitting ordinary citizens that was established by successive Democratic presidencies, beginning with the New Deal, turned the corner in service to the behind-the-scenes corporate puppet

---

[144] Deborah Davis, *Katherine the Great...,* (Bethesda: Zenith, 1987), p. 139; Alex Constantine, *Virtual Government, CIA Mind Control Operations in America,* (Venice, CA: Feral House, 1997), p. 36 ff. It's not just that advertisers ideologically disdain "advocacy journalism," as is often alleged. The truth is, the shadow government's control over the media by today – with far-fewer and more like-minded corporate news entities to manage – is lockdown total.

masters. Only Social Security and related Medicare remained on the table, their impact undiluted, but for pilfering of funds and threats of re-tooling.

The Reagan administration's adventures in Central America and in Iran-Contra, bringing two battlefields of choice together, as well as the ill-famed "October Surprise" that may have gotten Reagan installed in the first place, largely occurred *around* him, the strings pulled mainly by his mega-corporate aides in strategic posts. He was the perfect, tanned, avuncular front man in Washington, just as at GE.[145]

Just as, under the TV front man Reagan, the Middle East, Central American, "commie" and diaper-headed terrorist bogeymen converged, so under his successor, *mystery-agent* George H.W. Bush, the money-power (in the guise of S & L and BCCI money launderers), drug power, and old CIA assets and *patsies* in Panama and Iraq converged to accentuate a single, action-packed White House term. With *hush-hush* mind-control sex-slave fare thrown in as a kicker, implicating – improbably – the seemingly-bland-as-milquetoast senior President Bush, Ivy League scion and ex-oilman, *himself.*

The founding of *al-Qaeda* (meaning "the [data] base"), a CIA patsy cell useful for cats-paw fighting against the Russians in Afghanistan in the 1980s, brought Osama (*or Usama*) bin Laden onto the team and CIA payroll for the first time. Thus, the stage was beginning to be set for even more daring and dramatic operations probably already in view.

The Mujahadin, forerunner of the Taliban, was a radical Muslim militant group conjured to inject a loose-cannon, fanatical element among the religiously-staid Afghans as a foil to the anathema Marxist cult sponsored by the Russians.[146]

---

[145] Sheldon S. Wolin, op. cit., p. 156.

[146] *Independent Commission of Inquiry..., The U.S. Invasion of Panama*, (Boston: South End Press, 1991); Richard Labéviere, *Dollars and Terror, The United States and Islam*, transl. by Martin DeMers, (New York: Algora Publishing, 2000), p. 63 ff.

The $150 billion S & L bailout of the late '80s that launched the Bush recession and essentially cost the aptly-named "Poppy" re-election turned out to be by far the best bargain he ever cut us.[147]

So, just how much further from *"government of the people, by the people, and for the people"* could we possibly get? *Let's see!*

---

[147] Of course, everyone most likely knows by now of the babies-dumped-from-Kuwaiti-incubators ruse used to trick the public into supporting – no, demanding – the attack on fellow-thug George Bush, Sr.'s one-time best "friend" and dumped CIA asset-turned-defector-to-the-insufferable-Euro Saddam. See. Russ Baker, op. cit., p. 437.

Part 11 - **Millennials & Millennarians -** 1993-2012

The voters who elected Bill Clinton were no doubt disappointed, by and large, to find that, as with any other modern president, the amount of progressive government involvement and help with America's pressing problems from his administration, once in office, was quite limited, regardless of promises made. That was because, since the well-earned disgrace of America's powerful financial managers that swept Franklin Roosevelt into office, followed by the painfully-slow recovery with the help of government, the tide of money and benefit from government had reversed its direction, once more away from salaried workers, pensioners, and the poor. Now, the benefits accrued, as of old, *pell-mell* toward the coffers and balance sheets of the powerful.

And the powers-that-be dictated a continued wholesale movement of the country's money in *their* direction, no matter who was elected to the presidency or Congress. "We the people" were no longer in charge in any real way. If we had been, few, if any, of the paths taken or decisions made these last three or four generations would have been the same.[148]

As it is, it's sardonically amusing to read in a hundred treatises in this age about our "managed democracy" or "democracy in peril," or the "crisis of our democracy." My question is: *What democracy?* The parameters inside which the government can operate are today set by the "shadow institutions" that represent big money and actual power, no matter how few actual *Americans* are directly represented in the process.

And the *first-line* beneficiaries of the decisions made number one or two million individuals, tops, out of three hundred plus million Americans. *These* clients' true representatives are not in the government itself. Instead, *their* interests are represented by the Council of Foreign Relations, the Federal Reserve Board, World Bank, WTO, U.S. Chamber of Commerce, Heritage Foundation, Brookings Institution, AIPAC, CATO Institute, at a global level, Bilderberg Group, which many Americans may have never even heard of, plus a handful of other such organizations.[149]

---

[148] That's why Congress hasn't effectively blown its top at egregious power-grabs by the executive – they know the imposed limits and expectations. And, just in case Congress doesn't get it sometime, there's always the presidential signing-statement to fall back on, the despotic spark of the streamlined future Unitary Executive.

[149] David Rockefeller, proud arch-foundation member and plutocratic activist, describes the Council on Foreign Relations, the Bilderberg Group, and the Trilateral Commission frankly, from the inside, in his memoirs: *David Rockefeller, Memoirs,*

And, such are in business only to *get their way*. So then, isn't *that* simply the nature of "interest group or Madisonian democracy?" No, it's effectively *oligarchy*. And, as *single-sided* as it is, moving upward (*downward*) from Eisenhower's epiphany regarding the growing power of the "military-industrial complex", it is *authentic authoritarianism*.

Theoretically, the citizenry – the voters, or *hoi-polloi* – still *can* get their way on a selected issue. But, they have to decisively, as one, *rebel* against the wishes of the establishment and the relentless, strong current of propaganda, both blatant and subtle in the media, and *INSIST* – as they finally began to at the end of the Vietnam War, when the general and telling dissatisfaction was also shared by the troops in the field, who finally *just sat down* (or *stood down*, as modern parlance has rephrased it). But, *that* doesn't happen even once a generation – and the *real* "deciders" know it. The Constitution is window dressing. *It's their game now.*

It's their *show*. And we're their managed, needy but not too demanding, herd – *the sheep of their pasture*. And those *among them and among us* who speak up effectively with a different voice are called out, normally not by the leaders or even the police, but by the *system* that self-enforces comfortable conformance, today's *orthodoxy* of belief.

State terrorism can be useful, if a projected enemy, contrived or real, can be blamed for something. A decided public perception can thus be cultivated and massaged or shaped, as well as fear that permits the state to act in the way it desires – though highly objectionable otherwise – to alleviate the perceived threat.

Such was the shadow government's motivation for producing the sinister deception that was Operation Gladio in Cold War Europe (see Part 10, above). And *such* would seem to have motivated the FBI's apparent "*false-flag*" bombing of the World Trade Center, on February 26, 1993.

Curiously, according to an exclusive *New York Times* investigative report, published in late October, 1993, eight months after the incident it referred to, an Arab "terrorist cell" was shadowed by the FBI after its (the FBI's) construction of a bomb to detonate in order to destroy or seriously damage that complex. A member of the contracted group, claimed by the FBI to be an FBI plant, a former Egyptian army officer named Emad Salem, secretly taped hundreds of hours of involved meetings with FBI officials. In these recorded meetings, elaborate instructions were given to the group members involved, who were told by their handlers that a harmless powder would be substituted for the bomb's explosives, and that they were, in fact, only participating in a non-lethal exercise.

(New York: Random House, 2002), pp. 404-419. Congress has essentially conceded sovereignty to the most international of these groups.

Salem, after the fact, finding that the explosives had not been removed, turned the recordings in to the New York City authorities.

He testified that he, as well as the other Arabs, were shocked to discover that the FBI had failed to substitute the harmless powder for the explosive charge, and that the bomb actually detonated, killing six people, injuring over a thousand, and causing over half a billion dollars in damage.

Thus, the FBI's motivation and the intent of the group they later claimed to have been only "shadowing" were both placed in question.

According to the FBI, they had uncovered the terrorist cell's alleged planning weeks in advance and went along in order to track its progress and arrest the perpetrators, an explanation that seems to defy logical examination.

In any case, the incident was initially – in February – reported as a dangerous terrorist attack, and the public's attention was trained, at a minimum, in a fashion that could be useful to the FBI and U.S. authorities mounting a false-flag attack implicating Arabs as terrorists within the U.S. The obvious problem with the FBI's explanation, though, is a big one: if they were carrying out a sting operation, *why did they utterly fail to stop the attack?* Why, in that case, did they *let it happen?* And (while we're at it) why would they not themselves be prosecuted or brought to account *at least for that?*

The reporting or substance of the *New York Times* article was not repeated in the U.S. press *ever*, and Emad Salem was offered witness protection and half a million dollars to testify the FBI's way. Josie (or Guzie) Hadas, a long-established Mossad operative, was also questioned by the New York police for having rented the Ryder van involved in the attack for Arab suspect Mohammed Salemeh, but was not detained.[150]

Whatever motive or meaning could be postulated with regard to *other* high-profile violent acts of that period (Ruby Ridge, Waco, bombings in the Middle East, Africa, and in mid-air) would be sheer speculation in the absence of impartial investigation. But the *de facto* creation of a public narrative and conditioning thereby renders those incidents, too, worthy of some skepticism.

But, *to the contrary*, the Oklahoma City Murrah Federal Building bombing on April 19, 1995, and its reporting in the national media – totally at odds with earlier reports directly from the scene by the media in Oklahoma City –

---

[150] See Ralph Blumenthal, "Tapes Depict Proposal to Thwart Bomb Used in Trade Center Blast," The New York Times, October 28, 1993, p. A1; Ralph Schoenman, "Who Bombed the World Trade Center – 1993? Growing Evidence who Points to Role of an FBI Operative," originally in *Prevailing Winds Magazine*, Number 3 (1993).

seems to constitute a clear case of deliberate deception and disinformation, for whatever purpose, of at least the vast majority of Americans who would not have been particularly attendant to the early, locally-reported details of the incident.

For the first couple of hours afterward, local news stations in Oklahoma City reported *definitively* that a second, more-powerful bomb had been located and was being defused. This *second bomb*, on the east side of the building, was located after the blast of the infamous bomb inside the yellow Ryder truck parked on the north side had occurred, sheering off that whole side of the nine-story building. *And then*, it was reported, only locally, that a *third* equally powerful, undetonated, bomb had been located by the search units dispatched.

Oklahoma Governor Frank Keating *himself* reported on-air the finding of the second bomb, something he later denied, even though his report to the interviewer was (and is) recorded on tape. Within a couple of hours, word had come down from the national media that the single Ryder truck bomb on the north side had been the *only* explosive device present, and the local journalists and officials changed their reporting *at that point* to so state.

In the aftermath of the bombing, a number of demolition experts declared, after making a full study of the pattern of destruction caused to the building, that it was *in no way credible* that a single blast of the magnitude reported, or even of much greater magnitude, originating in the location indicated, could have caused such widespread destruction inside that structure.

In one section that was completely leveled, for example, the destructive force would have totaled a mere 27 pounds per square inch, insufficient to even apply stress. There would, in other words, have had to been other, pre-set, detonations on the inside *in conjunction with* the one the government (and compliant mainstream media) insisted – after the first two hours – was responsible for all of the damage.

"It had to have been mined," an ex-Green Beret Vietnam-era military demolitions specialist, who remained anonymous because he couldn't afford to risk his veteran's benefits, declared. "It couldn't have been done externally like that. Without cutting charges, there's just no way to do it,"

Benton K. Partin, a retired U.S. Air Force Brigadier General, long responsible for the design and testing of practically all non-nuclear devices employed by the Air Force, exhaustively researched the Murrah Building bombing and detailed his conclusions in a letter handed to each member of the U.S. House and Senate in May, 1995, a month after the blast.

"When I first saw the pictures of the truck bomb's asymmetrical damage to the Federal Building," he wrote, "my immediate reaction was that the pattern of damage would have been technically impossible without supplementing demolition charges at some of the reinforcing concrete column bases... For a simplistic truck-bomb of the size and composition reported to be able to reach out on the order of 60 feet and collapse a reinforced column base the size of column A-7 is beyond credulity."[151]

Oklahoma State Representative Charles Key noted immediately that the conclusions in what was reported changed dramatically during the morning of the incident, from before to after the national news media took charge of the story line. Upset by this major anomaly, he moved at once to launch a citizen-initiated grand jury investigation to determine the truth of the matter, something that is only authorized in Oklahoma and one other state.

For some time after initiating the procedure, though, he found the effort stymied by two obstacles. One obstacle was that officialdom and the press, both inside and outside Oklahoma, closed ranks to denounce his action and defend the altered official version.

The second obstacle the effort faced for a considerable time was a complete lack of funding.

When the Citizens' Grand Jury Investigation finally was set in motion, it came to pass that the numerous eye-witnesses to there being several other figures conspicuously involved by association with Timothy McVeigh, the lone active perpetrator charged, were all blocked by federal government lawyers from testifying. Timothy McVeigh, with limited assistance from Terry Nichols, was the lone official suspect. And that's the way it was going to go down.

When several documents emerged that seemed to indicate prior government knowledge of the attack, up to two weeks before, the government's response was to remain tight-lipped. But, apparently, the federal government quietly circulated a story that what had transpired, resulting in the *apparent* connection of others to the case, as well as indications of government fore-knowledge, could have been the existence of a sting operation, not to be interfered with early. Incredibly, the same story circulated by the FBI in connection with the world Trade Center bombing two years earlier. But, reportedly, no ATF – Bureau of Alcohol, Tobacco, and Firearms – agents were in their offices at the time of the blast. And, *once again, if it had been a string, the government utterly failed to block the deadly attack.*

It's just common sense to conclude, that the likelihood is that, for reasons of its own – unless it can be shown that someone else set off lethal blasts elsewhere inside the structure – *the federal government*, for reasons of its

---

[151] David Hoffman, *The Oklahoma City Bombing and the Politics of Terror*, (Venice, CA: Feral House, 1998), p. 1.

own, might have set off bombs itself simultaneously and strategically, elsewhere in the building. And, *for certain*, there was *something* the government desperately didn't want the people to know.[152]

Shock events seemed to many to almost fall on top of each other from the early '90s forward. Which candidate one may have favored in the presidential election of 2000, to cite a prime example, was a matter of individual preference. Regardless, the Chief Justice Louis Rendquist-led U.S. Supreme Court's shameless abandonment of the clear (but *inconvenient*) provision in the Constitution to be followed in the event of the sort of outcome faced, must be seen by anyone paying attention as equally, or even more *shocking*.

The Court's trashing of the normal procedure involving the binding nature of the state law – shocking enough to the Court itself to be declared *not* a precedent – was probably the only way the candidate favored by the shadow government could have prevailed. The ballot and voter qualification procedures employed had already tilted the election artificially in George W. Bush's favor. And the Court's decision simply sealed the deal, setting the stage for an unprecedented, and perpetually scandalous administration.[153]

But that democratic sovereignty (the creed's *government by the people*) was thereby *openly* usurped does not suggest at all that it hadn't been *less-openly* usurped by shadow institutions for some time – as we have seen that it has.

Supposedly, our civilization in particular pretends to rationality. Our much-touted creedal tenet of *"Liberty and Justice for all"* requires the unyielding pursuit of justice as *non-optional*, but to be served by uniform due process. As a norm, the best science available is applied in as clear-headed and impartial manner as possible, and witnesses are compelled to testify and are immunized as required.

Intentionally, all the stops of effort and exactitude are removed to reach a level of truth *"beyond a reasonable doubt"* whenever a crime is committed or a significant matter is in dispute.

Bur in the case of the notorious crimes committed on September 11, 2001, the illegitimately-anointed president, still in his first year, in accordance with a theory about a conspiracy apparently spun instantaneously to cover ("explain") the involved attacks, undignified by crime research and untried in any court, simply pronounced by *fiat* the establishment's designated suspects

---

[152] David Hoffman, op. cit., pp. x – xii ("Foreword" by Representative Charles Key). 374 ff, 453 ff, et al.

[153] See Jack 453 ff, et al.

[153] See Jack N. Rackove, ed., *The Unfinished Election of 2000*, (New York: Basic Books, 2001).

guilty. And a narrative was released *immediately* to attempt to put over on us this highly unorthodox *total abrogation of justice and the guarantees of due process*.

And, unbelievably – as *unthinkable* as such a dictatorial procedure would have been the day before, and as inconsistent with all aspects of America's creed we claim makes our system *different* and *better* – *practically no one raised a serious objection*.

In the wake of that galling, illegitimate *evasion*, close to everything the federal government of the United States has done ever since, overseas and domestically, has been in response or heavily influenced – *illegitimately* – thereby.

Among the results of that extreme folly, a sort of *national rapid-onset psychosis* were: 1) the illegal taking of almost 1.5 million lives, overwhelmingly non-combatants, in *unjustified* wars of vengeance and aggression, 2) the *unjustified* subservient truncation of our civil liberties (including the complete evisceration of the Constitution's Fourth Amendment (*security from unwarranted searches*), and 3) the decade-long co-option of our national agenda of much-needed governance. Plus, other serious related losses were suffered as a result, including severe economic and psychological trauma. Our freedom and our lives, and those of countless others, have been outright *stolen*, and *truth* has suffered a crippling, possibly existential blow.

Running all the attendant risks of violating perhaps the strongest taboo in our national culture, at least since discussion in public of abolition of slavery in the early 1830s, let us broach the subject of the *truth* in regards to the government and national media's telling of what actually happened on 9/11/01. And let's face it *head-on*, registering the logical possibility that the official narrative *could be* false and misleading. (Given the government's record at crucial points over the years, much of which is cited here, there exists plenty of precedent for that "possibility" and ample reason to entertain it.)

If we (government and individuals) have been responding, for nine years and running, to a narrative of events that is false, and thereby misleading, our tragic, earth shattering *responses* cannot in all truth be justified; they need to be repudiated and, in so far as possible, *corrected* before they cause even more undue damage.

As I will illustrate, the government/mainstream media narrative *doesn't fit or account for the known irrefutable facts* gleaned from the 9/11 incidents. That's why – even if it's fringy or disgraceful or a sacrilege to think this thought – *it cannot be what happened*. There are versions of what happened that are very much closer to fitting the known facts.

The crimes of September 11, 2001, are so vast and multifaceted that there are easily hundreds of different evidentiary paths and trails that can be followed into the thicket of what really happened that day. Some of them are surprisingly easy and clear, and some more technical. And nearly every one of them, if objectively followed, proves or strongly indicates the official story to be utterly *false*.

Which is why all possible pains have been taken by government spokesmen and the media to convince the public *not* the look closely at the actual evidence, to steer clear of even considering it – *in order to avoid a risky encounter with obvious implications*.

What if it turned out to be true that the government lied to us about what took place that fateful day, and was actually involved in producing it? What would that do to our view of our selves, our place, and our country? Answer: It would inform and prepare us to act accordingly, for one thing!

If the above paragraph expresses your thinking about 9/11 and the *bare possibility* that the objectors to the official story might be correct, then you are in good company! Polls show you might actually be in the majority.

On the other hand, much of the intelligent public, including some of our most-renowned and revered thinkers, such as Noam Chomsky and most of the thinkers and writers of *The Nation,* have taken to heart the government's more than subtle insistence that they stay away from seriously considering the case and they have simply *steered clear* of following and investigating the ample evidence for themselves having to do with what really happened on 9/11.

So, amazingly, many millions – including leading analysts and thinkers – have little or no awareness or knowledge of the courtroom-worthy evidence that conclusively proves that the government sold the public a lie and, beyond a doubt, is thereby shielding those individuals and programs responsible.

Access to virtually the whole, large, surprisingly comprehensible corpus of 9/11 evidence, gained and compiled by diligent researchers, many of them highly degreed and impressively experienced professionals, can be gained easily by *anyone* on the Internet, including references to many excellently-written (and argued) books, videos, and articles.

Thus, for my part, I won't try to offer here a panorama. Instead, I will lay out, straightforwardly as I can, a *single* evidentiary path that I believe can, by itself, reveal that the establishment's all-important version of events is completely untenable.

Indications are that the establishment narrative of 9/11 was 100% *shadow government* fabricated, tailor-made to suit the purposes of the background *powers-that-be*. There's *no* credible or primary evidence whatsoever, for instance, that there were *any Arabs on any airliners* that day. Known manifests contain *no* Arab names. There are *no* known surveillance camera shots from that day – as are routinely used to authenticate – of a single Arab entering any of the involved flights. Cell phones, 2001-vintage, have been conclusively demonstrated *not to work at all* above 8,000 feet of altitude. Even Barbara Olson's famous call has been reported by the FBI to have lasted "0.0 seconds."[154]

In as plain English as I can muster, the particular line of evidence I alluded to which could conclusively prove the official (and ubiquitous) narrative, seminal and essential to all that followed in reaction, false and misguided, is as follows:

Nanothermite is a super, highly explosive form of otherwise simply incendiary *thermite*, invented and produced exclusively by the U.S. military, usable as a spectacularly potentiated blasting agent. Its *super* effectiveness is due in part to the tremendously heightened heat levels its detonation produces and its rare capability to thus pulverize concrete and melt steel. Particles of this particular material were found in abundance by independent research scientists in four separate dust samples reliably obtained in the vicinity of the Twin Towers (#1 and 2) of the World Trade Center post-9/11/01.

Developed by the U.S. military, and only produced domestically in and accessible strictly from one or two U.S. military labs, *thermite* in *nano* form has only one conceivable use or purpose – the pre-set *controlled demolition* of mega-buildings and sites. That's the *only* conceivable reason quantities of *nanothermite* (extrapolated to have totaled up to 40 tons emplaced) *would or could* have been present in the prodigious dust from those enormous buildings.

Charges of the same material have to be *expertly* pre-set over days or weeks to make possible precisely the textbook example of total sudden onset *disintegration* of the targeted structures, from the roofs down, observed on 9/11. It couldn't have been dumped in haphazardly by crashing aircraft. Only *authorized personnel*, with access to the material as well as the buildings – *and not Arab Muslims* – could have placed the material there – *with but one intent*.

Now, the question becomes: *Who planted it, and who ordered them to?* Khalid Sheik Mohammed couldn't have done it. Osama bin Laden couldn't have. The crashing aircraft were but a ruse, the fires from their burning fuel incapable of producing heat levels anywhere near the close to 3,000 degrees

---

[154] See David Ray Griffin, *Debunking 9/11 Debunking*, (Northampton, MA: Olive Branch Press, 2007), pp. 87- 91; _____, *The New Pearl Harbor Revisited*, (Northampton, MA: Olive Branch Press, 2008), pp. 61, 87-94, 172-173, 313 n. 150.

Fahrenheit necessary to suddenly *melt* the steel support columns in order for them to all fail simultaneously.

It is true that other lines of evidence, if followed, might well produce evidence as compelling. But, officially authenticating (or disproving, for that matter) that the abundant substance found in the dust, identified as *nanothermite* by the eminently-qualified scientific investigators involved, really was so, could *disprove the theory of responsibility the government and media sold the public. And such an impartial test could, at the same time, establish 9/11 as the most spectacular (and devious) false-flag operation in all of history.*[155]

In the words of Dr. David Ray Griffin, perhaps the world's most knowledgeable and credible 9/11 scholar, "The evidence that 9/11 was an inside job is overwhelming (meaning that people inside the U.S. government or people they contracted or collaborated with were the parties responsible)." And, to repeat: such could be established or refuted by objective, open testing, if the government would agree.[156]

Occasionally, there are debates online between defenders of the official line and those pressing forward and defending the evidence, of one sort or another, of inside involvement in the 9/11 terror attacks or of non-involvement by Middle Easterners.

The national news media, on the other hand, far from ever debating the issue, very rarely acknowledge that any disagreement over responsibility for 9/11 even exists. The national media itself has *never*, not even at the beginning, questioned the official version of events on 9/11 at all, once it was laid out in the first day or so. And when any mention is made of those who *do* question and depart from the official line, the actual claims or evidence presented by the dissenters are never debated, or even mentioned – except occasionally in ridiculous caricature. And those making the claims are uniformly referred to as "idiots," "imbeciles," "nut cases" and worse, with the fact that they so claimed attributed to mental instability.

Nor are politicians, with one or two quickly disqualified and removed exceptions nation-wide, *ever* open-minded or conscientious in embracing this issue. As Griffin put it, "[A]lthough 9/11 was indisputably the most fateful event of our time, from which enormous consequences – almost entirely negative – have flowed, neither Congress nor the mainstream media have

---

[155] See Stephen E. Jones, Neils H. Harrit, Kevin R. Ryan, et al, "Active Thermite Material Discovered in Dust from the 9/11 World Trade Center Catastrophe," The Open Chemical Physics Journal, (2009), pp. 2, 7-31; Stephen Jones, Ph.D., 'Nanothermite", (DVD), 911TV.org, (2009).

[156] Truth is, unvarnished truth is itself taboo, and the plan to prevent its ravages is to dilute it in an ocean of contextual silence. Heaven forbid!

investigated the reasons provided by independent researchers from many professions for considering the official account false."[157]

No wonder – in one sense – that the media have faithfully parroted the government line, with all the fear and sad "news" that 9/11 and its consequences have generated. It's given them two wars, tons of troubling legislation, and nonstop statements by "patriotic" politicians and government officials, national and local. *It's all money in the bank.*

And it's no wonder that, since the very beginning, when questioners in Congress were encountering frame-ups and denunciations that invariably got them sidelined and some mysteriously *deceased*, politicians will steer completely clear and walk a mile out of the way to avoid being cornered with questions about the origins of 9/11.

As with *verboten* causes and issues in the past, families have broken up over 9/11 guilt, marriages shattered, employments ended. Accusations of bad faith and *delusional* thinking have filled the air at times. Yet, the controversy persists, *brash and bold*. And, due to its paramount importance and the strength and quantity of the evidence, *it's no wonder!*

But, there is *no statute of limitations on either mass-murder or treason.* From our standard context of daily grind, our *exceptional* nation-state, and the expectation of effective and representative government, that is the conclusion that one concerned enough to investigate almost inevitably reaches.

From the colder, more-detached viewpoint of the *shadow government*, though, it becomes more of a *management problem*, with what *we* would call an unimaginably *drastic* initiative, justified by its purpose in the larger and longer scheme of things. The deed and the spin, the false narrative pushed out of necessity aboard the public mind, all part of the message going forward. *Not* a crisis for them, just a long day's work, coming off acceptably, and *sold* as planned. Now, they have to stick with the (disproven) account to protect their own hegemony from unraveling and creating (for them) immense, unmanaged and unimagined chaos, opprobrium, and failure to attain their own special forefathers' *and their* dream.[158]

The *de facto* repudiation of America's *revolutionary* (and Revolutionary era) *creed* – with people having *freedom to control the government, being free from government control, all men (all people) created equal, liberty and*

---

[157] David Ray Griffin, *Debunking 9/11 Debunking*, p. 1; David Ray Griffin, *The New Pearl Harbor Revisited*, p. ix. A rich cache of information is readily available, online and elsewhere, for all concerned.

[158] Their forefathers' dream (and the goal of the Bilderbergers, etc.) the exclusive vehicle of the cadre of élite families (which, you'll note, the media never ask them to explain) is what George Bush, Sr., David Rockefeller, and others have enigmatically called the "New World Order."

justice for all, and *personal as well as national independence* – actually began with the hard-headed, bare-bones Constitution of the United States in 1787. The Framers of that pragmatic new compact were ready for business, not idealism. So, the *creed* the first young Americans memorized on their school benches and learned it set us apart, even then, went *underground.*

It, in effect, gave way to a republican elitist *freedom of association* Constitution, which made liberty and democracy a thing of the marketplace, *not* something participated in the same way by all. The animus that certain quarters have re-ignited against Abraham Lincoln of late probably had (and has) little to do with him being the president of the Union side in the Civil War. It might have more to do with him resoundingly re-launching in his Gettysburg Address the American *creed "rebirth of freedom"* Constitution (that author George Fletcher calls "the secret Constitution"). Some people who really don't want to share, are cynics, and despise ordinary mortals, share such hateful assessments of Lincoln. *Why?*

Were Lincoln's pronouncements *just words? No!* Because, people who act on them can pose dangers to elite power and dominance![159]

Thereafter, with the conservatives and *union-busting* elites back in power, our briefly revived revolutionary *creed* sentiment, which produced the later willfully-misconstrued Fourteenth Amendment, was driven right back underground, and began to re-surface again only with the *New Deal*, after the money power had thoroughly discredited itself, with Kennedy and the "New Frontier" and after multifaceted human rights movement of the 1960s, so *despised (that word again!)* by big money and *anti-creedal* interests.[160]

And then there came with a *thump* the baldly authoritarian *Bush v Gore* coup via Supreme Court *usurpation* and the resoundingly cynical sudden sleight-of-hand of 9/11, expressly designed to beat the *creedal* crap out of the American nation – to force the primal energies of America's dark side paranoia to resurface, as a control mechanism, with the designated *merchants of fear* at the power levers fronting for the *shadow government*. Shades of Jim Crow, the Red Scare, the days of rage, mobbing, and the *Know Nothings* again, complete with a conjured bogeyman in an unreachable cave harassing us like Genghis-khan from the ends of the earth.

And warnings from *On High* not to look behind the curtain or question 9/11!

---

[159] George P. Fletcher, *Our Secret Constitution, How Lincoln Redefined American Democracy*, (New York: Oxford Univ. Press, 2001).
[160] See Peter Collier and David Horowitz, *Destructive Generation, Second Thoughts About the Sixties*, (San Francisco: Encounter Books, 1989).

So, how has our induced national credulousness about the attacks on September 11, 2001, even *hurt* us? *Let us count the ways!*

First, the misbegotten overseas wars of "revenge" against the *un-guilty* – a demonized and stigmatized one-fifth of humanity, in fact, our brothers and sisters, fellow full and rightful human beings – *happened because we sanctioned them.*

If we hadn't gotten swept away in the post-9/11 hysteria that yelled out for revenge and totally bypassed justice and all semblance of the deliberative, unbiased inquiry process we claim as our national (*creedal*) pride, something that sets us apart and marks us as *exceptional* – those awful, obscene wars *never could have happened.*

And, two unsavory foreigners, raised to prominence by our own "security" agencies and elected leaders in the past, could never have been inflated out of all reason into *monsters* demanding holy patriotic crusades from us that caused to perish in agony and despair one and a half million mostly non-combatant, perfectly innocent people who previously meant us no harm.[161]

We all know inside that our leaders know that revenge for 9/11 is *not* the reason we're over there raping and destroying those alien countries. Our leaders, including inevitably President Obama, know the true story of 9/11. They just don't know that *we* know the *truth* is not *at all* as they billed it. So, to rehabilitate our sweet land, a land of peace and good will with a glorious national *creed* revered in every part of the world, we've got to tell them that we know, too – and that *the jig is up! We're no longer children! Prosecute the mass-killers – NOW!*

The horrible aftermath of Katrina simply showed that our government's resources and attentions were being devoted to looting and giving cronies license and not on serving *us*.

We can now see plainly played out yet again what has *always* happened when nakedly unconstitutional, long ago banished unrestrained *money power* is left in command of national finances – *ours in particular. Our independence is prostrated – sold, jeopardized, and compromised from within.*[162]

---

[161] For a sobering perspective, see David Ray Griffin, <u>Osama bin Laden, Dead or Alive?</u> (Northampton, MA: Olive Branch Press, 2009). The actual number of in-country deaths in the war in Iraq alone is at least 10 times any estimate quoted by U.S. government sources, currently being published as 1,316,000, based on the same scientific calculation used internationally, without a quibble, for deaths in all other wars. See emailtom@coxnet.com.

[162] One of the corporatocracy's motives for the war in Afghanistan is, without a doubt, maintaining control of the lucrative trade in drugs, behind only oil and arms

The fact that the BP oil spill could occur as it did demonstrates even more emphatically anew, what happens when *"We the people"* are marginalized beyond relevance by the *oligarchy* (the *shadow government* and their front men) who are making of our national life a *show* – an increasingly bitter mega-tragedy staged for us in lieu of freedom and opportunity, a lavish surreal matinee paradise for the few, all at our expense – *but for only as long as we let them.*

---

as an item of global exchange, with that country growing 93% of the world's opium. Following the effective eradication program, production plummeted to just 185 tons in 2001, then soared under U.S. occupation to over 6,000 tons and rising – a more than 30-fold increase by 2007. Impoverished Afghan farmers and merchants ("drug lords") together in that country only receive 2% of the amount of the eventual street price for the drug. From there, a series of middlemen launder the mounting profits (over $200B annually) through "offshore banks" controlled by the major Western banking houses, in Cayman Islands Switzerland, and elsewhere immune from investigation, factoring prominently, along with mega-dealings in arms and petroleum in keeping their ledgers highly profitable, despite shocks and blunders, and them astride the world. See Michel Chossudovsky, *America's "War on Terrorism,"* (Pincourt, PQ, Canada: Global Research, 2005), pp. 224-236); U.N. Office of Drugs and Crime, Afghanistan. Opium Poppy Survey, 2004; Wikipedia, "Opium Production." Russia offered in March, 2010, to eradicate the entire Afghan crop by spraying; the U.S. declined, stating that doing so would harm the local economy too much.

Part 12 – Starting Today – We Begin to Personify Our Creed

A decade and a half ago, shortly before his death, Christopher Lasch wrote that democracy in America was *declining* in the hands of managerial and professional elites who lack a connection to traditional American civil and social (i.e., ordinary American) values. Lasch was onto something, but far too mild in his assessment.[163]

The corporate managerial types who are routinely given reign over the management of our many-faceted national affairs today, in cabinet and sub-cabinet positions, are in no way even self-respecting *surrogates* for the general citizenry of this country, any more than National and American League All-Star teams represent student athletes. In fact, our actual rubber-meets-the-road governmental administrators, and even most of our elected officials, resemble most of us to about the same extent the *commissars* under the Soviets represented or resembled the proletariat.

And, that's not too surprising. (Remember: our intelligence services, in particular the CIA, were imaged at the beginning of the Cold War to resemble Soviet Intelligence *more than it did itself*). Ours is a *professional* system of governing – not ignoring the fact that the professionalism of *these* professionals has not been encouraging when it comes to *results*. That's because *we're* not their bosses.

For "democracy" is just a word to throw in speeches these days, like parsley flakes thrown in a salad. There's little or no resemblance between the outcomes most people hope for and *want* from our system anymore and the policies that emerge to govern us. In fact, people seldom even think in terms of what they would *like* these days, because they don't expect anyone with any power to take any of their suggestions or requests seriously. And, in stark contrast to the preferences expressed by foundations and big contributors, they *don't*.

"We the people" rarely can get our way, even when we overwhelmingly agree on a preferred outcome (as on the "*public option*" largely favored by the public and blithely left out of the 2010 final Health Care bill, or as with the Afghan and Iraq Wars – to name just a couple of current examples). They just expect us to soon forget and renew *their* charters to "serve," anyway. Only rarely do things go otherwise.

---

[163] Christopher Lasch, *The Revolt of the Elites and the Betrayal of Democracy*, (New York: Norton, 1996).

Overwhelmingly, we are the ruled, and *not at all* the rulers of our land. *The oligarchic élite rules – the funding, sanctioning and information-monopolizing shadow government behind the scenes.* Even the all-too-rare victories for the people are engineered to mainly serve the *corporatocracy's* interests. It's become operationally *their* country, and our needs are not their first, or even second, concern.[164]

To cite the most flagrant example: Immediately after 9/11, the White House ordered its Environmental Protection Services Secretary, Christine Todd Whitman, to send word to the recovery workers that the air at Ground Zero in lower Manhattan was safe to breathe – *under the circumstances, a prosecutable criminal act of felony lying*, resulting directly in the eventual deaths of several times the number of persons who died in the attacks themselves. A question many holdouts cling to regarding 9/11 is: "But, would people in the government kill 3,000 of their own citizens?" The obvious answer is: They killed far more than *that* almost within hours afterward. So, *yes, decidedly*.[165]

Then, in the shadow of *that*, there were the anthrax attacks by posted letter. Conceivably, the purpose of those was to warn sometimes-wayward members of Congress to stay the hell in line and not question the official line on things. The sniper attacks after that simply kept people on edge.

As have the string of purported terrorist attacks since, all (if you think about it) having the same characteristic *grade B sit-com think-tank situational planning-room* quality and type casting air about them, faintly mirroring *Operation Northwoods, Gulf of Tonkin, Operation Gladio, the WTC attack 1993, Oklahoma City, and with more than a smidgen of likelihood, Khobar Towers, London, Bali and Madrid, U.S. Liberty, and U.S. Cole* before. Even the 1985 Leon Klinghoffer *Achille Lauro* outrage. *Is* Al-Qaeda, deeply evil though it be, *still in fact* a protected asset of U.S. intelligence?[166] Sometimes, even *conspiracies produce evidence and witnesses*. With *so many* known

---

[164] But, to each his own. Former CIA global political analyst Patrick E. Lennon, in The Twilight of Democracy, (New York: Doubleday, 1995), did not lament that democracy was in crisis or endangered, but that there was entirely too much of it and it needed to be eradicated, to get the bumbling elected office holders out of the way so that the managers alone could manage business and government backup for maximum return and unbridled efficiency. Ivo H.

[165] Daalder and James M. Lindsey, two former Clinton staffers, in America Unbound, (Washington: Brookings Institution Press, 2003), praised the post-9/11 Bush administration for embracing exactly that policy prescription globally.

[166] Interview with Michel Chossudovsky, *Global Research*, July 20, 2006.

instances of public deception, wouldn't it be *amazing* if *all of these* were, to the contrary, *absolutely straight-up as advertised?*[167]

After the 1993 World Trade Center bombing, there was an official investigation and a grand jury issuing indictments. Not so after 9/11/01. The FBI began an investigation, but was ordered to stop by the White House. FEMA, followed by NIST (National Institute of Standards and Technology) conducted research into causes of the World Trade Center building collapses, under strict administration guidelines, steering away from any possibilities besides impact of planes and fire, a mandate they have been unwilling to abandon.

All the while, questions and evidence from citizen investigations have mounted; but all legal venues have remained effectively closed to 9/11-related investigatory matters and actions. Serious questions of the official story have been, to say the very least, discouraged and stigmatized. *Why is that?*

Instead of a point of view extolling open-mindedness and earnest inquiry – supposedly, the hallmark of American *democracy* and jurisprudence (the search for *justice*), all the persistent questioners have heard in response to their questions and evidence regarding 9/11 is, "That's absurd!" or, "You're crazy!" or, even, "That question is sacrilegious! Have you no respect for the *families?"* – which are not real *answers* at all, but just the rude intrusion of another false hypothesis meant to sidetrack. Because, they *have* no answers! (As I recall, the establishment has tried that same approach in the past, with Galileo.)

As I have amply – though cursorily – highlighted, stealth, violence, deceit, and fear-mongering, victimizing the poor and increasingly constricted middle classes, have been mainline products of the nation's government at home in recent years.

Meanwhile, treachery, bullying, and a transparent double standard have been the hallmark of U.S. actions abroad, especially away from the cameras.

For the sake not of our nation, which has repeatedly cringed at the infrequent revelations of what was really going on (as at Abu Ghraib and Guantanamo), and as with the all-too-rampant "collateral damage" of bombings, check-point decapitations of whole carloads, and street-sweep

---

[167] Kurt Haskell, Detroit area attorney and former federal employee, reported hearing and seeing in the departure waiting area of the Amsterdam airport at Christmastime, 2009, the later-identified young Nigerian bomber's arrival before the crucial flight, accompanied by a well-to-do Indian-looking man arguing to get him aboard the plane without a passport. U.S.-Israeli-designed (or MI-6) terror attack frame-ups and deceptions are rife, and not to be discounted as a strong possibility by alert citizens today. See James Hufferd, "Is Another False-Flag Provable?" 911Truth.org, January 12, 2010.

exercises. To say nothing of terror attacks delivered antiseptically from around the world by drone, ferocious mainline battles wasting populated areas filled with the old and the halt who couldn't get out, as at the silenced metropolis of Fallujah.

And echoed in all of the horrible *PTS cases* owned up to in the face of persistent ridicule by our own, daily *ordered* to do what ours, of all countries, isn't supposed to do or ask them to do to other human beings.* *And for what? For whom?* Do you and I actually *benefit* from the gory, visceral fatal muggings and disgraceful holings of people – little children, grandparents, lovely women and gentlemen as pain-prone and human and innocent as *we and our friends?*

Do such things that we all want to hide our face from and ignore actually *protect* you or me? True, if these victims love their country and want to protect their neighbors and families, such killings might help protect our troops, personnel, and bases that are senselessly and illegitimately there to pursue violent means to whatever clandestine ends (including simply grabbing what doesn't belong to us first).

But no, the profiteers and beneficiaries of all of that are not *us*, though beneficiaries and profiteers *there indeed be – at unimaginable taxpayer expense!* And their business ends, extremely remote from *our* purposes, are indeed among the reasons 9/11 was concocted and done – *the "new Pearl Harbor"* envisioned and called for in 1998 by the neo-con conclave calling itself the "New American Century."[168]

And, for instance, if the Iraq and Afghan Wars were indeed to lower the price of gasoline a little for us, those wars are certainly an expensive and inefficient way of going about it.

Brigadier General Smedley D. Butler, the outstanding Marine who foiled the American fascist plot to oust President Franklin Roosevelt and replace his administration with a friendly (to the business elite and the major bankers) dictatorship, published a little book in 1935 entitled, *War is a Racket.* In it, he warned of the role of lucrative profiteering in provoking and supporting modern-day warfare. "I spent 33 years in the Marines, most of the time being

---

[168] The Project for a New American Century, "Rebuilding America's Defenses: Strategy, Sources, and Resources for a New Century," p. 51. For two embedded journalists' sobering account of the carnage caused and encountered on a daily basis by regular U.S. combat soldiers involving civilians in Iraq, see Chris Hedges and Lala Al-Aian, *Collateral Damage, America's War Against Iraqi Civilians*, (New York: Nation Books, 2008); See also Ralph Lopez, "Wikileaks Soldier Reveals Orders for '360 Rotational Fire' in Iraq," "Op-Ed," June 17, 2010.

a high-class muscle-man for big business," he wrote. "I was a racketeer for Capitalism."[169]

Jeff McMahan, in his study, *Killing in Wartime*, convincingly makes the case that taking human life in that context is no better or more defensible than is murder. Killing in a war zone might be justified as self-defense; but then, what were you doing crashing into harm's way there, anyway? In my novel, *Homeland: A Comedy*, I had one of the characters propose an effective means of ending war.

Which is: have a universal compact agreeing that any country that attacks another country must give up its top leader for public execution within 60 days. Any violating country that failed to do so would be the object of a universal trade boycott, bringing wrack and ruin until it did. Period. It's an idea, at least. (And no country would ever make war on another, so that the penalty would never need to be exacted. For instance: would the U.S. have invaded Iraq if George W. Bush would have had to relinquish his life for the privilege? I, for one, don't think so). Other forms of politics would just have to do. As Smedley Butler succinctly put it in his little book: "*To hell with war!*"[170]

To the American public's highly suggestible (intimately well-known) mind, the slightly forbidding *half-baked plausibility* of the official theory of what happened on 9/11 proved irresistible. People love reading between the lines and letting their *adult* slightly risqué minds go where they've been asked *not* to go – or, in this case, draw a conclusion they've been asked *not* to draw.

They had been *asked* to conclude simply that "the radical Muslims [note: *not* radical Arabs, but radical *Muslims*] attacked us because they hate us for our freedom." Which makes utterly no sense! "Maybe a small child would believe that," many Americans might think, "just as they believe in the Easter Bunny!"

So, the question for the masses automatically became not, "Then, *who did* attack us?" but, rather, "So, *why did* they *really* attack us?"

Now, of course, the average citizen has heard of the concept "*blowback*," a fancy way of saying that if you wrong someone, they just might hit you back in some way. Of course, the average citizen might also be, however dimly, aware that the "*blowback*" concept was postulated by rogue former State Department analysts or investigative reporters, not on the best working terms

---

[169] Brigadier General Smedley D. Butler, *War is a Racket* (1935), (Port Townsend, WA: Feral House, 2003).

[170] Jeff McMahan, *Killing in War*, (Oxford: Oxford Univ. Press, 2009; James Hufferd, *Homeland, A Comedy*, (Joshua Tree, CA: Progressive Press, 2010); Smedley D. Butler, op. cit., p. 45.

with the current government, and probably a bunch of left-wingers. And he or she will probably be aware also that the concept of *blowback* is not embraced by current administration officials, who maintain the long-term stance that the United States is innocent of any sort of wrong-doing overseas.

But still, the average citizen wasn't born yesterday, and is a grown-up. And gets the general idea of those *radical Muslims* agreeing with that leftist notion of "*blowback*" and attacking us because, *in their deranged minds*, America has transgressed against them in the Middle East – meaning fanatical Muslim terrorists of that sort probably *would* seek vengeance by way of a cockamamie plan like 9/11.

And, at least at first glance, it seems like *they might!* So, there *is* a certain *plausibility* to that *blowback*, revenge idea, giving the implicated Muslim terrorists a motive – *if you don't look too closely at the evidence and crime scene (and most people don't!).*

And, as the *psychological operations* specialists in various relevant agencies of the U.S. government know – being no doubt the leading experts in the world on the U.S. public mindset and its manipulation, once the public at large reaches a conclusion about something, in the absence of something really dramatic to change that conception, *you've got them!*

The problem is that the superficially arrived at generalized mental picture the public has about what happened on 9/11 does not fit the *evidence,* which, the public is, however, not apt to study at any length.

That mental picture in no way explains, for instance, the large quantities of super-explosive *nanothermite* present in the prodigious dust from the buildings. It does not explain the hundreds of testimonies of those present in the buildings of multiple powerful explosions from *below* the floors they were on. It doesn't begin to explain how those buildings collapsed suddenly and completely, straight down at near free-fall speed, neatly into their own footprints, or how 47-story Building 7 (the Salomon Brothers' Building) similarly collapsed late in the afternoon of September 11, (even though it had not been hit by an aircraft). And, there are a hundred other things that are scientific impossibilities or don't fit if that's the explanation imposed.

And so, the conventional wisdom, exuding an air of public relations plausibility – as the planners of the crime most certainly knew that it would – is clearly wrong, *a useful dead end, and the basis for a taboo to be jettisoned – like that about abolition.*

The same endlessly resourceful *corporatocracy* (*not* just the often Keystone Cops-like visible U.S. government) spouting the rhetoric of democracy, basic equality, fairness, and financial assistance for countries that desperately need it, is just as heavily involved in other aspects of global operation besides bombings and military shock-and-awe.

For instance, *unheard-of* amounts of money are funneled through secret channels to productively aid selective candidates in poor countries' elections who give assurances they will comply with U.S. State Department imperatives. And leaders of countries disfavored by the U.S. in certain regions are warned not to make their economies too prosperous or their governments too successful or popular, or the U.S. will see to their ouster, assassination, or suicide.

It's what happened to Aldo Moro in Italy. It's what happened to Mohammed Mossadegh in Iran, and more recently, the active force in the "Color Revolutions" (in Ukraine and other former Soviet republics). Before that, reportedly, Presidents Arbenz (Guatemala) and Torrijos (Panama) fell prey.[171] And, it's what was slated for Ahmadinajad in Iran, when the CIA quietly funneled huge amounts of cash to his election opponent. Then, frustrated by its utter failure to derail the process, the U.S. cried foul and "stolen election," after the results turned out *precisely* as predicted in terms of percentages by *all of* the numerous prestigious prior polls – including by a respected American polling company. The U.S. media's unanimous declaration that the election had been stolen was shameless, though not unrevealing.[172]

Also Hugo Chavez in Venezuela (where a first ouster attempt failed), and other democratically elected presidents in South American countries presently displeasing to the *shadow government*. Aristide (Haiti) and a raft of Caribbean and Central American leaders were thus overthrown, and *perhaps* even Rabin and Sadat. *It wouldn't be out of character and nothing has happened to make the CIA change.*

The CIA established *al-Qaeda* and the *Mujahadin*[173] itself in Afghanistan, introducing radical Islam to dislodge the more-pedantic moderates and push along the crack-up of the Middle East, in preference to Soviet control. There's evidence that the Israeli MOSSAD created Hamas among the Palestinians, for similar reasons. It is presently reported that virtually all Afghans believe the U.S. is – *true to form* – funding the Taliban.[174]

---

[171] John Perkins, *Confessions of an Economic Hit Man*, (Berkeley: Berrett-Koehler, 2004), pp. 72-73, 158-161.

[172] Personal conversation with Dr. Ismael Hossein-Zadeh, Professor of Economics, Drake University, author of *The Political Economy of U.S. Militarism*, (New York: Palgrave-Macmillan, 2007), repeating points stated publicly in a speech at Drake University, Des Moines, Iowa, November, 2009.

[173] John Perkins, op. cit., pp. 96-97.

[174] See Hosane Zerousky, "Hamas is a Creature of the Mossad," (Global Outlook, Summer 2002), citing Zeev Sternell, historian, Hebrew Univ., Jerusalem. Hamas was set up as a puppet to unify Israeli opinion on the militant side, while Israel brutally suppressed Arafat's moderate Fatah movement.

All of the particular *puppet or patsy terrorist organizations* in the Middle East follow essentially the deceptive pattern of sponsored patsy terrorist groups founded by the CIA to battle Communists with diabolical false-flag ops in Europe under Project Gladio. Meanwhile, what is deceptively called "Free Trade Policy" (as though is promoted human freedom) can only benefit the *comporatocracy* of the wealthy countries, by driving local agricultural and other kinds of producers out of existence when they can't compete successfully in their own markets or simply provide food – instead of introduced cash export crops – for local people. The programs that cause the most tumult in poor countries' economies are most often introduced stealthily, under deceptive rubrics, as forms of "assistance."[175]

In the Middle East and elsewhere (formerly, most notoriously in Latin America and the Caribbean), the U.S. has earned ill-favor by not only overthrowing elected leaders, but by propping up and assisting the worst dictatorships and human rights violators in exchange for giving the U.S. *corporatocracy* free reign to corrupt and pillage along with them, as the best of buddies. *Objectively, a troublesome country!*[176]

So, while hacking down the economies and democratic politics of distant countries, has the American *shadow government* been at least bolstering its own? Hardly. The *corporatocracy* that literally bought and paid for the American government, including the press, made its continued support contingent on their virtually eliminating the protective regulatory culture in all of its aspects, subjecting the populace to all the hazards of all the corporate mega-menagerie run amok wide open, sheets to the wind with power. Outsourcing jobs and plants became not just tolerated, but *subsidized.* Meaning if you, a true and rightful "citizen," really wanted to have a job or a chance at a job, it's probably best to book passage now to Kuala-Lumpur.

And the whole perennial regime ruling America and, by extension, looming over the world like a terrorist colossus standing over a house of cards, was (*is*) the unconstitutional – (no, *doubly* unconstitutional) – Federal Reserve system, relinquishing the country's (the *nation's*) intended and hard-

---

[175] John Perkins, *Confessions of an Economic Hit Man*, op. cit. Naomi Klein, *Shock Doctrine, The Rise of Disaster Capitalism*, (New York: Picador, 2007), goes into more detail revealing how many convoluted, Machivellian plots that are hatched unfold to deliver unsuspecting, struggling economies and nations haplessly into the "market capitalist" basket of the U.S and its hard-knuckle, play-for-keeps leading-nation allies.

[176] Even this very day (in late June, 2010), reading between the lines just a bit in the transcript of Secy. Hillary Rodham Clinton's remarks delivered to the OAS (Organization of American States), the U.S. seems ominously to be preparing for corrective intervention into several "wayward" Latin American countries.

won independence to a culture of bottomless, endless, boundless, inevitably uncontrollable – and totally unnecessary – hellish and ruinous *debt*.

There isn't enough money available in the United States to fund the ongoing, massive, *unnecessary* purchase of the American money supply at interest from the foolishly entrusted private business interest. So, much of the money to in effect *buy* our money and pay the cumulative interest must come from lenders, investors, *controllers* and *owners* abroad.

What makes the federal government's arrangement to buy money from the Fed (which makes it in the sense Hershey's makes chocolate, except out of *nothing*) *unconstitutional?* Again, the Constitution's Article 1, Section 7, says that the *Congress* has to coin and issue the money. Additionally, since 1935, there's been the U.S. Supreme Court's decision in the case of *Schechter Poultry v. U.S.*, which requires explicitly that Congress not abdicate or transfer to others its Constitutional functions.

Hence, the Fed is *doubly* unconstitutional, and someone needs to call Congress on it to shut down the arrangement and emit the U.S. money supply as needed, without cost or borrowing, backed by our capacity to work, supply, and create – being as we're sufficiently productive for the purpose.[177]

Our government, as set forth in the Constitution, is designed explicitly to work for us (*"We the people..."*) and for us to be, ultimately, *self-governing*, an *independent nation*. But the Federal Reserve System fundamentally governs us today, perhaps conferring with select others in doing so, not completely unilaterally, by expanding or contracting the money supply. To make our funding of our freedom of action contingent, and either easy, or a living nightmare, depending.

The Fed, in other words, does not at all fit the intentions of the Framers of our Constitution both because it controls us – *not we it* – and the Constitution forbids its existence. And, to cap it all off, the Fed "does not allow the public into its meetings [unlike, normally, the Congress], does not publish transcripts of its meetings [unlike, for instance, Congress], and is responsible [only] to itself for its own budget."[178] And its presence and our government's (and, by

---

[177] Webster Griffin Tarpley's analysis in his book, <u>Surviving the Cataclysm</u>, (Joshua Tree, CA: Progressive Press, 2009), is incisive, but not particularly consistent. Starting on page 57, he suggests – not unreasonably, that the Federal Reserve System be forced "to open a main street lending facility." It definitely could help to provide needed credit to ordinary business people and small lenders! Problem is, less than ten pages later, starting on page 66, he leads off with "End the Fed – End Wall Street Bankster Rule," an incomparably better idea.

[178] Thom Hartmann, <u>Unequal Protection, The Rise of Corporate Dominance and the Theft of Human Rights</u>, (New York: Radale Books, 2002), p. 40.

extension, *ours*, by our taxes) unending obligation to it severely compromises our *independence* as a sovereign nation.

What we need to undertake to fix this monstrous problem could be called an *import substitution policy for money*, with Congress itself faithfully returning to its precious mandate.

Of course, there has always been a pushback in America against the customarily *dominant* power of the forces that, by design or effect (that is, by a sort of unintended collateral damage, or so they say) have tended to push us ever farther in the direction of inequality – inequality of station, inequality of respect, inequality of opportunity and the ability to earn a living, inequality before the law. When is the last time you heard of someone prominent in America being convicted and incarcerated? True, Martha Stewart was. But she was sent up by vengeful fellow dignitaries, her actual guilt much in doubt. Bernie Madoff. Right. Because he fleeced *billionaires*. Enron execs? Hardly. They only fleeced the janitor and family man cubicle dweller and the ordinary California taxpayer. A plurality of the nation yelled and hissed at them. That was all. (Some still wait for Ken Lay's re-emergence.) Bush, Cheney, and the gang, you fill in the blank. No prosecutions. No official inquiries. They walk, amid barely even any tongue clicking. "We look forward, not back." (And what Mr. Obama may have meant is, they did what they were hired to do).

Meanwhile, the guy who held up a pizza deliveryman and stole change and a medium pepperoni, jail time. Was he black or white? It matters; statistics prove it.

September 11, 2001, the largest single crimes in U.S. history, not criminally investigated. Due process, like so many other security systems on that one day and having to do with that day, *inoperative. We're mad (insane)! To hell with the Constitution!*

Don't you sense that unequal protection is *no* protection? There's no justice without truth. Not in Mogadishu. Not in Pyongyang. Not in Teiran. *Not here.*

Lincoln tried to re-introduce us to equality and democracy as real propositions. President Jackson did so as far as even he could. FDR took the meaning of our nationhood to heart and moved the pendulum back in the midst of national suffering and rejection of the financial oligarchy.

JFK tried to narrow the gap. The women's suffrage and civil rights crusaders woke us up to the possibility. Despised southern abolitionists pushed back in their day. Some of the above have paid with their lives. *A luta continua!*[179]

Another way the *corporatocracy* very inordinately influences and straightjackets American life to suit its own precepts is through philanthropies. The highly concentrated private wealth that owns so much of America plays an enormous supplemental – more often the *primary* – role in financing a dizzying variety of beneficial funds and charitable institutions. And in many cases, this private *philanthropy* is an essential, even uniquely indispensible, resource for the charity or institution involved.

It follows, however, as is frequently pointed out about *governmental* support and assistance, that *the power to fund is the power to control.* And in the case of philanthropic foundations, it is well to note, the power to control quasi-public institutions that shape American life and thought is, though not illegitimate, *extra-constitutional,* serving the interests of super-wealthy and usually deeply conservative masters, and not necessarily the public.

Because, while the Constitution endows the common treasury with oversight and authority to appropriate "to promote the *general* welfare," the character of our system, as envisioned in our founding documents, did not foresee this *mega-private* means of exerting control over institutions and programs, mainly because such inordinately large concentrations of wealth hadn't accrued yet when the Constitution was written.

The sources of great wealth involved are, of course, not *just* or primarily those of families, but perhaps even more so those of great corporations. And such sources of funding are not strictly public-spirited, but strive to shape everything to promote *their own* interests, which in most cases is no doubt their primary motive here, as in all else.

Accordingly, they gainsay and, from their platform as benefactors, strive to shape our daily experiences in a thousand ways. Hence, private foundations – super-wealthy, usually deeply conservative – touted and praised by public information specialists on their payrolls, are again as much bane as benefit to most individuals, and even more so to whatever semblance remains of democratic control of our society.[180] *Much has changed since 1787!*

---

[179] Benjamin DeMott's book of readings for students, *Created Equal, Reading and Writing about Class in America*, (New York: Harper-Collins, 1996) was a pushback in this sense.

[180] Joel L. Fleishman, *The Foundation, A Great American Secret*, (New York: Public Affairs, 2007), pp. 33 ff, extols foundations for their generosity of spirit. Robert L. Payton and Michael P. Moody, *Understanding Philanthropy*, (Bloomington: Indiana Univ. Press, 2008), pp. 155 ff, goes farther and suggests that philanthropy – by the moguls and through the cutthroat boardrooms – actually endows the funding of

Bigotry on the public stage is – *praise be!* – no longer silently countenanced. But, in private actions, beyond the public school and lunch counter door, the old 1890s doctrine of *"separate but equal"* still thrives. Freedom of association, in matrimony and socially, is upheld. But, in housing and the reactionary world of private (separate) schooling, even in religion, the old and mean rule today keeps millions inept at dealing with, even knowing and properly respecting, each other.[181]

Journalist Tom Wicker's book, *A Time to Die*, constitutes reflections spurred by his personal involvement with the 1971 Attica prison riots in New York, evocative of injustices seared into his consciousness by his southern boyhood. His book is an indictment of America's world-topping incarceration rates and the unequal justice meted to blacks and other darker-skinned citizens still relevant today.[182]

As everyone knows, but some still try to deny or defray acknowledging, even before "America" was fabricated under a stolen sovereignty, it was staked out and erected on stolen land. That native America was subjected to genocide is provable, but supposedly mitigated by paeans of praise for the *noble warrior, pagan religionist, first conservationist, patriot,* or by denigration (*savage, crude sociological* or *biological unit*). As in *"he's a survivor and wise, better than we are in some respects,"* or *"he was a dirty, ignorant primitive, unworthy of this great land, hardly worthy to survive in it at all."*

Elizabeth Cook-Lynn, a professor-emeritus and member of the Crow-Creek-Sioux tribe, decries the posturing and patronage alike, and the exploitation, bullying, and hate crimes against persons of native ancestry and culture. Citing numerous examples, she baldly accuses the general American community of both genocide and ecocide against the original inhabitants. As we know, Ward Churchill was pilloried and his very *Indian-ness* ridiculed and attacked for raising many of the same points without sugar-coating them, and then daring to exercise his *inalienable* free speech rights honestly. We prefer, it seems, to only look forward.[183]

Darker-skinned people are still not wholeheartedly embraced as brothers and sisters here (let alone, of course, in targeted resource-lands overseas), to

---

benefits with moral guidance and tone that normal people just couldn't endow them with!

[181] Jonathan Kozol, *The Shame of the Nation, The Restoration of Apartheid Schooling in America*, (New York: Random House, 2005), documents and laments this continuing phenomenon. But then, Barack Obama's election to the presidency bespoke the desire of many millions among us to be fair – a more than good sign.

[182] Tom Wicker, *A Time to Die*, (New York: Quadrangle, 1975).

[183] Elizabeth Cook-Lynn, *Anti-Indianism in Modern America*, (Urbana: Univ. of Illinois Press, 2001), p. 185 ff.

the extent that "illegal alien" (not simply "suspected violators of the law of entry" for accurately designating *some*) has been superimposed to replace "Hispanics-origin Americans" wholesale in many people's minds. We don't know what to do with even the more compelling legal claims made by darker skin persons, no matter how deep their roots.

Reies Tijerina led militant Old Spanish residents in a movement centering on a remote court house in northern New Mexico, not terribly long ago, to recover lands allegedly stolen from their ancestors by newly-arrived Anglos after New Mexico was annexed in the late 1840s. Considered a gadfly, he was finally convicted of destroying Forest Service signs and sentenced to imprisonment for three years.

At a hearing, one of his law enforcement antagonists was asked if he would like to see Reies "put away permanently". The officer said he would. In the process of his legal arraignment, Reies Tijerina was sent to a mental facility and, according to some accounts, lobotomized. Possibly not; but at least, subsequently, he was a much milder fellow, with not too much more ever heard from him.[184]

Suffice it to say that American women are still waiting to attain the reward of pay equal to men for the same or equal work, 80 cents on the dollar being the currently-relevant ratio.[185]

*   *   *

So: Given such a stunning record of resoundingly "un-American" acts and facts as one finds at the core of our nation's history through the present-day, reeking and dripping blood through every single generation of our charmed but checkered existence, what is one to conclude? Please honestly note that this is not just reverse *cherry-picking* that might produce a few questionable examples to not be overly proud of, but a pretty consistently dismal legacy.

With that awareness, how can anyone *still* say, for instance, that insiders sufficiently in control of the U.S. establishment and government *would not* have been responsible for anything as *bad* as deliberately choreographing and staging 9/11?[186]

I would have to conclude that such a reflexive, immediate blanket dismissal without answer, by individuals, repeatedly, of evidence, proving as

---

[184] Richard Gardner, *Grito! Reies Tijerina and the New Mexico Land Grant War of 1967*, (New York: Harper & Row, 1970).

[185] Borgna Brunner, "The Wage Gap", Infoplease, 2010.

[186] See Stanley Cohen, *States of Denial, Knowledge about Atrocities and Suffering*, (Malden, MA: Polity Press, 2001). More to the point, Martha Stout, *The Paranoia Switch, How Terror Rewires Our Brains and Reshapes Our Behavior*, (New York: Farrar, Straus, and Giroux, 2007).

much is, above all, a well-earned tribute to the government's/establishment's *stellar* domestic and overseas propaganda operation. U.S. propaganda of self-praise echoes through our textbooks and schools, from the pulpits of churches, throughout the print and broadcast media, and is distributed widely abroad by outlets such as VOA (Voice of America).

Endlessly repeated messages from the same operate in many cases after awhile – *after years* – subconsciously. Such messages are not, by and large, about 9/11 at all, but are deliberately designed to make it sound and seem to people who don't research things much that our beautiful and wildly-popular national creed, codified and featured in this book, is *descriptive* of our nation's and our government's actions and practices on a daily basis.

"We are the good guys – unquestionably, *always* the good guys," so goes the consistently inculcated message. "Underhandedness, dishonorable conduct, cheating, deceit, mistreatment and abuse of women, children, minorities, small animals, are all exclusively the province of others, not us, with *very few* exceptions." *And if you still think that, you'd better read this book again!*

Another glaring shortcoming is that trivial entertainment is given *far* more attention – allegedly to sell more cars, shampoo, dopey pills, annuities, panty-liners – than *details* of anything vital to our lives. And alternative views of such information as is presented are cited only when their purveyors – who are not always exceedingly credible themselves -- can be made to seem foolish or flop-down delusional.[187]

That we Americans now have *"the worst quality of life in the developed world – by a wide margin"* is actually well-documented, and not even all that surprising, given our schizophrenic thoroughgoing abandonment of our own avowed very wise and good cardinal principles and Founders' guiding lights. Debt slavery and stress over realistic fears of ruin are just two very bad aspects.[188]

So, let's see just where we stand now in relation to the various tenets of our purposeful national *creed*:

1) <u>Freedom to control the government</u>. No matter what the American people want or need our government to do today, we possess little or no power to bring it about. We are *not* a democracy, but, practically speaking, an *oligarchy*, as I have abundantly demonstrated.

---

[187] Chris Hedges, in <u>*Empire of Illusion*</u>, (New York: Norton, 2009, laments the "precipitous end of literacy and the symptomatic triumph of spectacle in America" as heralding the dying of culture.

[188] See Lance Freeman, "America: The Grim Truth", <u>Information Clearing House</u>, April 8, 2010.

2) <u>Freedom from governmental control</u>. For most of us, the *corporatocracy*-controlled government, via the masters of psychological manipulation it employs and its airtight control over the major information media, conditions our thoughts, responses, and daily choices. In its effectiveness, it almost certainly equals or surpasses the creation a few decades ago in another venue of the compliant "*homo sovieticus.*" It likewise effectively shields the public from exposure to items of news and views designated taboo.

3) <u>All men (all humans) are created equal</u>. We have seen what a crock that has become, both in terms of our relationship with the law, and in our largely "news"-conditioned attitudes. Among other meanings, "*All men are created equal*" is a repudiation of the priority or special power of some blood lines over others.

4) <u>Liberty and justice for all</u>. *Must I say it again?*

5) <u>Personal and national independence</u>. Due to the subordination and perhaps psychic terror exercised over Congress and, now fairly-reliably, the presidency, our glaringly unconstitutional and hazardous monetary arrangement has effaced and nearly erased both our national and personal *independence*. (Such need not be done via any super-secret deal involving Mexico and Canada. It's already done through monetary virtual suicide.) *Here*, the love of money truly and clearly *is* the root of all evil. The only question left is, how long are *we* willing to permit such a totally hamstringing, unnecessary control exercised over us by a long-established private conspiracy to continue?

President Andrew Jackson stated: "If Congress has the right under the Constitution to issue paper money, it was given them to use themselves, not to be delegated for individuals or corporations." *Toward what end?* Abraham Lincoln said it would be in order that "money will cease to be master and will become the servant of humanity." *We the people*, as human beings, *real persons*, deserve no less.

*   *   *

I believe that we do still have a real choice. In order to avoid continuing to operate as utter (and *obvious*) *hypocrites*, we can begin today to start living as the *personification* of our matchless uniting values – our *creed*. And *demand* and *continue to demand* nothing less from our government. And, I *guarantee* we will thus meet with unprecedented success. The world will naturally be drawn to us as *respecting all* (not least, *ourselves*) and emulate us.

Or, alternatively, we need to devise a new creed to better suit the reality of our long-term behavior.

Here are a few suggestions for such a new *creed*'s tenets, if we decide to go that route:

By hook and by crook

Bunk and bombs alone

Separate but unequal justice (injustice)

We don't give a damn/God loves us anyway

Just shut up and follow orders

The end justifies the means

      8) _____.

      9) _____.

      (We'll need lots of rationalizations…!)

And now, at last, to the remedy: I believe that practicing and requiring the consistent practice by our government of the five true tenets of America's national creed will bring about as sudden and revolutionary a turn-around to the overall fiscal and social tremors and shortfalls of the United States as a healthful infusion of Vitamins A, B, C, D, and E could bring to a human organism deadened and degraded by a lifelong steady diet of junk food and Secretary Donald Rumsfeld's *Aspartame*.

Note: this creed is nothing exotic. It is what we already loudly proclaim we believe in.

And, I believe, along with our founding Forefathers – no sentimental fools – who devised every facet of America's revolutionary creed – (DEMOCRACY, FREEDOM, EQUALITY, JUSTICE, & INDEPENDENCE) for all – that we can make our national creed live in this world, and can only thus derive its true and intended benefits!

Adel, IA, USA,

10/01/2011

INDEX

PROGRESSIVE PRESS

In bookstores, online, or on sale from ProgressivePress.com

Also by James Hufferd: *Homeland: A Comedy.* Our presidential puppet agrees to sell the USA to 'The Company' outright. $11.95.

Six by Webster Griffin Tarpley
9/11 Synthetic Terror: Made in USA – by a network of moles, patsies, killers, corrupt politicians and media. The MIHOP Bible. 569 pp, $19.95.

Barack H. Obama: the Unauthorized Biography. Obama the puppet of Brzezinski and Goldman Sachs, a product of Chicago corruption. Richly detailed profile of today's finance oligarchy. 595 pp, $19.95.

George Bush: The Unauthorized Biography. Vivid X-ray of the oligarchy dominating U.S. politics, with a full narrative of GWHB's long list of crimes. 700 pp, $19.95.

Obama – The Postmodern Coup: Making of a Manchurian Candidate. Obama's advisors are radical reactionaries. Astute insights. 320 pp, $15.95.

Surviving the Cataclysm, Your Guide through the Greatest Financial Crisis in Human History. The financial crises of recent decades. 668 pp, $25.

Just Too Weird - Bishop Romney and the Mormon Takeover of America: Polygamy, Theocracy and Subversion. Incredible background on Mormonism US fascism and the GOP. 278 pp, $10.

History
Gladio: NATO's Dagger at the Heart of Europe - The Pentagon-Nazi-Mafia Terror Axis. Wet works and false flags keep Europe a US colony. Leaders murdered, movements subverted, death squads rule. 484 pp, $16.95.

Terrorism and the Illuminati, A 3000-Year History. "Islamic" terrorists are tentacles of western imperialism – the Illuminati. 332 pp, $16.95.

Subverting Syria: How CIA Contra Gangs and NGO's Manufacture, Mislabel and Market Mass Murder. "Rebels" are the Pentagon's secret weapon. 115 pp, $7.49.

The Nazi Hydra in America: Suppressed History of a Century by Glen Yeadon. How US plutocrats launched Hitler and built today's police state. Fascists ran both sides of WWII. "Deserves to be widely read." – Howard Zinn. 700 pp, $19.95.

Psychology, Brainwashing
The Rape of the Mind: The Psychology of Thought Control, Menticide and Brainwashing. Conditioning under fascism and corporatism. Self-defense techniques. 320 pp, $16.95.

The Telescreen: An Empirical Study of the Destruction of Consciousness. How mass media brainwash us with consumerism and war propaganda. Fake history, news, issues, and reality steal our souls. 199 pp, $14.95.

Conspiracy, NWO
Corporatism: the Secret Government of the New World Order. Corporations control all resources on this "prison planet." 408 pp, $16.95.

Final Warning: A History of the New World Order. In-depth research into the Great Conspiracy: the Fed, the CFR, Trilaterals, Illuminati. 360 pp, $14.95.

Conspiracies, Conspiracy Theories and the Secrets of 9/11. German bestseller explores conspiracy in history, biology, and on 9/11. 274 pp, $14.95.

The Money Power. Two books in one: *Pawns in the Game* and *Empire of the City.* The divide-and-conquer plan of 20th and 21st centuries. 320 pp, $12.95.